About the Author

The author lives quietly in North Essex with his wife, Gill and, at the age of 70, he decided to write a book about the hundreds of unusual events and accidents which have befallen him from his birth to the present day. After leaving school at the age of 15, he worked in a printing works, an architect's office, gravel production and heavy earthmoving. Although semi-retired, he still finds time to try and kill himself – accidentally, of course.

Dedication

I would like to dedicate this book to the following people who have had to endure my mishaps:

To my wife Gill, who, for over 46 years, has sometimes watched me have an accident and has also nursed me back to health by issuing supportive grumblings.

To my sister, Brenda, who protected me from bullies in my early years and who also reminded me of some of the incident details and who also cried with laughter at some of my stories.

To my mother, Joyce, who must have had a few heart attacks as she watched her little boy becoming damaged and who stopped herself from throwing me out of the window.

To all the people who became wrapped up in my incidents whether they knew it was my fault or not.

Michael Sarling

THE ACCIDENT BOOK

100 Ways to Keep Calm and Carry On

AUSTIN MACAULEY PUBLISHERS™

LONDON • CAMBRIDGE • NEW YORK • SHARJAH

A CIP catalogue record for this title is available from the British Library.

ISBN 9781528920629 (Paperback)
ISBN 9781528963145 (ePub e-book)

www.austinmacauley.com

First Published (2019)
Austin Macauley Publishers Ltd
25 Canada Square
Canary Wharf
London
E14 5LQ

Disclaimer

Before you read my book, I must protect myself from being taken to court by you, the reader, just because you tried to recreate one of my stories. I must insist that you do not try out any of my adventures and then blame the outcome on me.

Please don't try them!

The last thing I want to happen is that you recreate one of my stories and then you get yourself killed and then take me to court and stand there in the dock with an elderly person wearing a white wig looking on and accuse me that it was because you read my book that you are now dead.

Please also note that my ideas on current Health & Safety procedures are only my own and not generally accepted by accident claims insurers. Unlike me, try to stay safe and keep out of trouble!

I hope you enjoy my book.

A Dictionary Explanation of
My Events

Accident (noun) Something bad that happens that is not expected or intended and that often damages something or injures someone (Done that, been there).

Incident (noun) An event that is either unpleasant or unusual (Done that, been there as well).

Adventure (noun) An unusual, exciting and possibly dangerous activity, such as a trip or experience, or the excitement produced by such an activity (Done that, been there, as well, as well).

And these events often cause:

Adrenaline (noun) A hormone produced by the adrenal glands during high stress or exciting situations. (Got through gallons of the stuff).

**My method for pulling out a nail from an
asbestos roof using a crowbar.
Scruffy the dog looks worried for some reason**

Contents

Preface

My wife Gill was washing up in the kitchen when she heard a thump and crash coming from the bathroom upstairs. She instinctively knew that I must have slipped out of the shower while I was cleaning it, but even so as she was walking up the stairs, she shouted, "What have you done now?" Entering the bathroom she found me lying on the floor with one leg over the loo and a pair of 'Y' fronts over my head. My left foot and ankle was turning shades of red and blue and I was laughing.

"I really do think I should write a book about my accidents, because if I find them funny, then others might?" Gill looked down on me and asked why I had a pair of underpants on my head. "Well, the spray I was using to clean the shower was getting up my nose, so instead of getting a face mask, I just grabbed the underpants. They have two holes for the eyes and the nose and mouth are covered." Gill looked down on me in disgust and I said, "The pants are clean!" and then she also started laughing.

My wife often calls me Mr Beige and I have never woken up one morning and thought, *Today I shall do something exciting or dangerous* or *Today I shall harm myself* or *Today I am going to be reckless*. My adventures have just happened without much planning or thought and all I have wanted to do was to get through life and survive. I just wanted to live a quiet life and do a normal job, but it just hasn't turned out that way.

Why did I finally decide to write this book? Well, my sister Brenda has Multiple Sclerosis and is in a nursing home. Whenever I visit her I usually tell a story from an event in my life to amuse her and to cheer her up. One day she remarked that I should write them all down because she thought other people might be interested to read about them, "OK, I'll do it," I said.

A book slowly formulated in my mind so I started to list down all the accidents and unusual incidents that I have been involved in and when I got to a few hundred I decided to stop and have a re-think. So I reduced the list down to about 100 to keep the book from becoming too boring. This book is not intended to be the story of my life (that could well be boring) but it sets out to give the reader an overview of some of my accidents, incidents and adventures that I have endured through (mostly) no fault of my own.

I have always attempted to be safe and careful in everything I do but despite this caution, it does not seem to have turned out that way. The reader may decide that these 'episodes' have been caused solely by my own inability to travel through life without being an idiot. This may be true and I really must try harder to stay out of trouble for the remainder of my life. However, I am also writing this book now, just in case I do not survive for too much longer.

Not all these events have happened to me as some have occurred when I have just been in the vicinity. I now take this opportunity to apologise to those people affected because probably, my close presence may have been the cause of their suffering.

I have attempted to write this story on a sort of timeline, but I have also split it up into blocks of subjects which may not follow a strict timeline. This may be confusing but all will hopefully become apparent as you read on.

I have been fortunate to have been interested in most things around me and have also been involved in a few hobbies so together with my unusual profession in earthmoving has brought me into many different situations which have been the cause of some of my stories. Let me give you a taster of a few of them.

After 8 hours of being held hostage and negotiating my own release I was finally able to drive home for tea.

The lightning bolt went through my eye, down my body, sparked off my elbow and hit the guy standing next to me. Night came quickly.
The shotgun pellets were being gouged out of my legs by the nice doctor and I was 'ouching' a bit when the nursing sister shouted at me, "For heaven's sake, the women in this ward are having

babies and are not making as much fuss as you – now keep quiet!"

Something went crack when I hit the ground and it was not my new riding hat, so what was it? "Gill, my neck hurts."

Have I wetted your appetite for more? I hope so.

When you read on, you may get the impression that I am a bit accident prone – really! I can't believe it. Whenever my neighbour Jill hears the clatter of a ladder or the whine of a chainsaw, she phones to let my wife Gill know that she has fuel in the car and is ready to take me to hospital.

However, I do seem to have an unlucky/lucky syndrome which means that I am unlucky to have these occurrences but really lucky that they were not more serious. I imagine that I have a guardian angel who likes to have a bit of fun with me just to see how I react to an unusual predicament and to see if I can get myself out of trouble.

I have decided to write this book by changing the names of companies that are still trading and people that are still alive just to protect the innocent – and the guilty.

Many of these incidents occurred long before the health and safety mind-set that we have today, where, if anything goes wrong, it is never your fault and you can usually gain lots of money by taking Tom Dick or Harry to court. There were no social workers to jump on parents if they saw that little Jonny had a bruise and teachers could discipline their pupils with sticks and plimsolls. Policemen and park keepers could clip a lad round the ear and parents could smack their kids. Times have changed for the better but I do think we have gone a bit too far and one thing that nobody can do is to change history. So as you read this book and exclaim that some of the situations are against the law – that's today and not yesteryear – thank goodness.

Just one other thing, you may feel as you read on, that I am making all this up. Honestly, my stories are all true and in some cases I have even dumbed down some of them. I have also left out quite a few effs and blinds to keep it nice for the little ones to read.

Anyway, I hope you enjoy reading about my adventures but please stay safe. It's probably best if you do not try any of them yourself! – But if you do – KEEP CALM AND CARRY ON!

Chapter 1
A Quick Life History

To enable you to understand the following stories in the sort of timeline thingy, I will give you a quick history of me. I was born at home in Hornchurch late 1949 and I went to a primary and secondary school in Hornchurch Essex. I hated every single minute of it. This was caused by the constant bullying from the other kids and the teachers and the fact that the teachers only taught the intelligent ones at the top of the class. They did not seem to care about any others which included me of course. In 1962 my family moved to Dagenham as my father had become a manager in a newsagent shop. Dagenham is sometimes looked down upon by the middle class people, but we found the natives were very friendly and down to earth. As soon as I was able I did a paper round in all weathers before cycling 5 miles to my school in Hornchurch.

Being a newsagent in Dagenham, my father came into contact with many Ford Motor workers who regularly went on strike. One day he came home and we laughed out loud when he told us that the WOMEN had gone on strike. "They won't last a day," we said. They recently made a film about it called *Made in Dagenham* and those women changed the world.

After leaving school I worked for a local printer for a year and then a house builder for two years. I then worked for a gravel company for 6 years and then an earthmoving contractor for 28 years. After that I became a self-employed earthmoving consultant. I am now semi-retired after 54 years of full-time work.

My many hobbies are explained later but I was deeply involved in horses for 35 years and aeroplanes for 12 years. I have lived in Essex all my life. I lived in Hornchurch until I was 12 years old, then in Dagenham for 12 years, Brentwood for three years and now I have lived in Braintree over 40 years. The

Sarling or De Salyng family has been in Essex since around the year 800 (Great Saling, Stanford Rivers, Kelvedon Hatch and Romford) so I am carrying on with the Essex boy tradition.

My family consisted of my father Cyril, mother Joyce, elder sister Brenda and younger brother Peter. Mother got skin cancer in the late 70s and was treated and is still with us today at over 90 years old. Unfortunately, father passed away with the big C when he was only 61 years old. Peter then passed away with the big C at the young age of 46 (when a year later my bother-in-law, Tony, passed away with the big C, also aged 46). And then my sister contracted Multiple Sclerosis. Hopefully I will take after my mother for longevity and last a few more years.

I am lucky enough to live in a house with some land and stables and I also fly a Cessna 172 light aircraft. Gill, my wife, and I were married in 1974 but were not blessed with children and this has enabled me to afford these material possessions as we have never had to be the Bank of Mum & Dad. Hopefully, I will be able to appreciate these luxuries for some time unless my guardian angel decides to abandon me, in which case my final accident will probably require me to leave this earth.

Me – on the right – wondering why Dad and Mum were trying to kill me

Chapter 2

Early Beginnings and a Foretaste of Things to Come

The early 1950s was the best possible time for a little chap like me to be born. Road traffic was rare and soft toilet paper was becoming available (I did not like the shiny Izal bum scratcher). Grownups had just been through a long period of trying to avoid being blown up by Herr Hitler, so the post-war peaceful conditions allowed them to let kids do as they pleased on their own and with minimal supervision. I mean, anything a kid got up to then was safer than playing with an unexploded bomb! Everything is relative! (The unexploded bomb appears in chapter 36 and guns from chapter 55!)

We were not really aware of child perverts but we were always told not to talk to 'strange' men. In addition there was no such thing as the dreaded HEALTH & SAFETY and shopkeepers would sell a small child anything from fireworks, razor blades, penknives, paraffin and even nitro methane. They assumed that a small boy would use his own common sense when handling dangerous things. This produced an environment in which great adventures could be performed by children.

I was born with yellow jaundice and crying. I cried constantly for about three years and it was not until many years later that I discovered that I was allergic to wool. Mum used to wrap me up all warm and snuggly in woollen clothes. Wool underwear, wool jumpers, wool shorts, even later on, wool swimming trunks. Scratch, scratch, itch, itch – tearing myself to bits, but Mum said I had to keep warm and toasty. She freely confesses that on one occasion, she seriously considered throwing me out of the bedroom window to stop me crying. If she had, I could have logged it as my first flying lesson.

Dad later said that I should toughen up – In that dress??

I also had a cough. Not now and then, but a permanent cough. Hack-hack, cough-cough, hoop-hoop, I went. Mum took me to all the best doctors and even a trick cyclist (Psychiatrist) who told her that I would grow out of it. I 'grew out of it' when I was about 10 years old. During a recent pilot aviation medical I was asked to blow into a cardboard tube for a lung function test. Hopeless! The doctor asked if I had had a long-term cough when I was young! "Yes," I said. "Yup, you have reduced lung power due to coughing a lot when you were developing." Well, I never!

Chapter 3
Attempting to Alter My Facial Appearance

I love milk and I still do and my theory is that it makes strong bones – see later accidents. At about 18 months old I was wobbly trotting along on the concrete path outside our house with my usual teat stuck onto a glass bottle of milk, when trip, smash! In the face, blood everywhere, panicking mother, loud adult noises, doctors, plasters, the works.

Then about three months later, I was in the same place but with no bottle with me this time (Mum had learnt not to allow me anywhere near a glass bottle). Trip – nice soft landing into the chain-link fence with a piece of rusty wire running up between my top gums and lip, blood everywhere, panicking mother trying to unhook me, Dad with wire snippers, loud adult noises, doctors, plasters, the works.

Our doctor told mother, "A bit higher up and it may have killed him." Up into the brain probably? Since that accident, I have always had wonky teeth.

Afterwards, Dad studied the whole of the chain-link fence and found that the only piece of wire sticking out was the piece that I had discovered. Well wasn't I good to find that bit! It could have been dangerous for someone otherwise.

Our garden was full of interesting hazards

Chapter 4
Early Experiments with Drugs

Grandma Sarling lived with us at home and occupied the front room. She lived and slept there and often had her friends in for (many) drinks and a natter. Her health problems required her to have certain pills, but definitely not sleeping pills for some reason and our family doctor insisted that he would not give them to her despite her requests.

A few months after the wire up the mouth accident I contracted mumps from my sister Brenda and was feeling poorly. Mother walked across the road to the telephone box and called the doctor. (Doctors came out to you in those days!) The doctor who came out was a locum and not our usual family one. He examined me and prescribed some mump pills and wrote out a prescription. As he walked back down the hallway he was called in by Grandmother. She asked him if she could have some sleeping pills as she had run out of them. He duly wrote out a prescription for her.

Mum asked Judy (our next-door neighbour's 9-year-old daughter) to go down to the chemists to get my prescription. As she passed down the hallway she was called in by Grandmother. "Be a good girl and get these pills for me but don't tell the others."

Judy came running back and gave Grandma her pills and my mother, my pills. Mum then gave me a couple of pills and waited for me to get better. I went to sleep. After a few hours mum noticed I was very asleep. Dad came home from work and thought I looked a bit too limp, so mum went over to the phone box to speak to the doctor. He said sleepiness was normal with the pills. "But," she replied, "he's like a rag doll."

"He shouldn't be like that," said the locum, "I'll come straight round to look at him."

When he turned up he examined the bottle of pills and upon finding MRS SARLING written on the sleeping pills instead of M R SARLING written on the mump pills, there was a panicking doctor, mother and father screaming, shouting, and a crying Grandmother, doctor smacking me, pumping chest, pouring strong coffee down my throat, and in the end a kill or cure – Purple Heart drugs.

Early the next morning I slowly came round only to then leap out of my cot through a drug-induced haze into the fire place and then cracking my head open. Blood everywhere, panicking mother, loud adult noises, doctors, plasters, the works. It was also my first try at flying without wings.

First attempt at flying goes wrong

Grandma was immunised against mumps with all those pills she had taken, but she never got to sleep that night.

Chapter 5
First Swimming and Drowning Lessons

I had survived until three and a half years old when I was being looked after by Mrs Ward (they were our next-door neighbours with a mum, dad and 12 kids!) She was a well-built and obviously fertile lady and was washing up in the kitchen keeping an eye on me from the window. I was standing next to their 2-metre-deep fishpond looking at the goldfish. She looked up and saw me standing there, she looked down and looked up again and I was gone.

I really do remember seeing the goldfish swimming past my eyes, upside down, when suddenly much to my disgust, I was hauled out of the pond by a screaming Mrs Ward. She must have covered the 20 metres in seconds flat and for a big lady, that was a feat in itself.

It must have been a heart-stopping moment when she looked and saw the soles of my sandals disappearing down into the murky water...They filled in the pond after that!

Examining fish close up

Chapter 6
Egg Head

Just before I went to primary school my mum took me to Harrow Lodge Park about a mile away from our home, to play on the swings and things. I had seen the bigger boys having fun on the climbing frame which was a cube of steel poles a bit similar to scaffolding and about 10-foot high. Mum told me not to climb very high but I had other ideas.

This climbing frame looked a lot like fun and at one time I saw a boy slide down the angled stay at the corner. After a bit of climbing in and out of the tubes, I decided that I would try sliding down the stay but to go one better and do it upside down. Hanging on by my legs, I carefully eased myself into the upside-down position ready to slide down. It did not occur to me that, had I achieved such a feat, how I would extract myself from this upside-down position at the bottom of the angled stay.

I needn't have worried about such a thing as somehow I let go fore and aft and fell onto the concrete, cushioning the blow by landing on my head. My mother recalls that she watched in horror as I fell 10-foot headfirst onto the concrete. Absolutely no blood anywhere, but silence until I came round and heard a panicking mother, loud adult noises, rushed to hospital, doctors, plasters, the works. I had a bump the size of a chicken egg for some time. I did try to analyse what went wrong but never did find out except that it was a totally prattish thing to do in the first place. I was also attempting again, to fly without wings.

Chapter 7
Primary Skool

Little did I know that from my first day at school and for the next 10 years I would be bullied unmercifully by the big boys. I was always small in stature and I was therefore an obvious target for big, lumpy lads who needed to exert their superiority and found it fun to take it out on me.

I don't really remember my first day at school as events overtook me in the shape of the class bully fairly soon after. He would find me every morning as I walked into the playground and get hold of me. He would then explain what physical injury he would inflict on me after school and that 'I had better watch out.' This from a 5-year-old!

I made sure I sat at the back of the classroom so I could not be stared at by him, but he often looked round at me and mouthed some threat. All day the only thing I could think of was how I could escape after school without him catching me. During playtime I tried to get in with some other children so that if he thumped me, the others might turn on him. It mostly worked but sometimes he would catch me on my own and then I would be thumped and kicked.

Sometimes I escaped before him, sometimes my bigger sister Brenda would protect me but sometimes he caught me and gave me another thumping. Inexplicably, on occasions he would leave me alone completely, having issued his treat early in the morning. I had worried all day and planned my escape only to be left alone. I learnt later that these were the tactics the Gestapo used during the war to terrorise their victims further. He was an expert and it just shows how evil little children can be.

My schoolwork suffered badly and I was not even considered worthy of taking the 11+ by my teachers. I was glad to leave at the age of 11 to go to my new school and get away from him; however, things were not a lot different there.

Chapter 8
Life Between 5 Years and 10 Years

My life outside of primary school was absolutely perfect for a small boy. I had three great friends Philip, Geoffrey and Steven Ward (remember the next-door neighbours?) Philip was a year older, Geoff was my age and Steven was a year younger. We four boys were allowed to do whatever we wanted as long as our parents never found out.

The picture of innocence

The gang building a den covered from head to foot in a film of black soot – me sitting on the left of the old boiler

Happy Days

Weekends and holidays would find us over Harrow Lodge Park. We would leave home early and head to the park. When we got there our mission was to climb the trees, catch sticklebacks and water snails, steal birds' eggs, sail our model boats on the pond and generally have a good time. We had to be a bit careful of the parky (Park Keeper) who had a dark uniform and a peaked cap. He would control the park like a military camp and woe betide any boy who was found up a tree or doing anything that he did not approve of. He had complete authority to shout at you and hit you if you answered back. We never told our parents if we got into trouble as we would have received a smack from dad if we did.

We always had a matchbox full of things such as Mercury. This could be obtained from a broken thermometer and it is shiny liquid metal which could be separated into little balls and then brought back together again. We now know that it is a very hazardous heavy metal and is highly toxic but we never intended to swallow it, just play with it – we had too much common sense…

The perfect plaything

This was a relatively accident-free period of my life with only the usual childhood illnesses, bumps, scrapes, cuts and bruises to deal with. However much the gang tried, we never really hurt ourselves. We always looked forward to the lead up to Guy Fawkes Night. Not so much for the fireworks display on the night but the lead up to it.

It all started when we were messing about with penny bangers placing them under stones and seeing how high we could blow them up. The thought occurred to us that if we cut open the bangers then filled something larger and tightly pack it with gunpowder and then set a fuse, we could blow up bigger things. We got hold of a spent casing of a fizzy firework like a Mount Vesuvius and packed it with gunpowder. Then we forced a fuse in the top. This took up about five penny bangers' worth of powder. We took it down the bottom of our garden, lit the fuse and stood back – quite a long way – rather fast. The bang was fantastic! But the problem was that it had used up five bangers and it was over in an instant. It was fun, but not too much fun.

Further thought was required. Now a tuppenny banger was twice the size of a penny banger and made the same bang as our five-banger one, so we needed some more thought if we wanted a bigger bang. Old biscuit tins were about one foot square with tight lids and readily available from the grocers. If we could put a tuppenny banger in a tin but hold the tin down with a heavy weight, we might be able to blow the tin apart. We chickened out of putting the heavy weight on the first one and it just blew the lid off. However, the next one we held down with a lump of heavy iron. Now that was a big bang! It blew the tin to bits with great big bulges in the sides. We must have blown up quite a few tins before we got fed up with playing with gunpowder.

Taking sensible precautions

The Ward kids had some fish tanks in a shed and we filled these up with toads and frogs and then found insects and spiders to feed them. We used to watch the frogs catching the insects. From catching fish, snails and all sorts of wildlife, we learnt about nature first hand.

Our next experiment was to find out how flat a halfpenny would become if we placed it on a railway line after having been run over by a train. This was a simple experiment and an ideal place was at the pedestrian crossing on a local branch line. We could walk onto the railway lines, put our ears on the rails just like the Red Indians did, and then place a halfpenny on top. We would then wait for a train to go past and then search for the flattened coin. Most of them disappeared into the track ballast, but some we found completely flat and as thin as paper. Once the experiment had been concluded, the next one had to be performed. And so life for me outside school was always exciting.

VERY
FLAT
HALF PENNY

It cost us a halfpenny every time!

Chapter 9
Big Boys' School

My secondary school was Hylands Secondary Boys School Hornchurch (now demolished). On the first day a northern teacher wrongly called my name out for the first time as Starling and I corrected him by saying it correctly. He asked me if my nickname was Spuggy as that was the local name for small birds where he came from. For the next four years I was only known as Spuggy.

My father thought that being sent to an all-boys school would toughen me up after my persistent bullying and crying during primary school. (It did not seem to occur to him that I was OK when I was not at school).

Ready for big boys school

So the day dawned when I turned up at Hylands. Apparently, it was normal for the bigger boys to introduce the new starters into the ways of the school by placing their heads down the toilets and pulling the chain and then de-bagging them. This was great fun for them and I assumed it was to 'toughen us all up'.

However, there was no actual Gestapo-style terrorising as the bullying was totally random and quick. This came from both the teachers and larger boys. Most of the teachers were male and had been in the forces during the war. This meant that they did not stand any nonsense and operated the school like an army camp. Discipline was strict and consisted of the cane, the gym slipper and the high-speed wooden blackboard eraser. ('High speed' as it was launched towards a wayward boy in class, causing instant obedience and bruising.)

Our PE teacher was a very fit, short, stocky man who we assumed had been a sergeant major in the army. His name was Mr Powell (behind his back his nickname was Bucket) however, he had other methods of discipline which had no bounds to the size of the boy. Slapping caused us to have large red hand marks all over our bodies and encouraged us to leap over the wooden horse with great gusto. Boxing was another punishment. If he did not agree with something a bigger boy did or said, then it was in the boxing ring he went, complete with gloves. He would show the rest of the class how to box and then lay out his opponent. Luckily, I was never forced to compete against him but I did watch the methods he used and it must have stuck somewhere in the little grey cells because I needed them later on.

Although I was bullied lightly, I will always remember the day in third form when the teacher came in and asked a boy called George to leave the classroom. He was bullying first, second and third-year boys so he was an expert at it. The teacher explained that they had found out about him and that the best way to stop him was for us to sort him out. He recommended that a few of the bigger boys lured him behind the cycle sheds after school and then after they softened him up a bit, then we smaller boys could finish his education. After all my suffering, it was like Christmas had come early. He was then called back into the classroom but no one told him what was in store.

His adjustment to normal life was carried out with much glee especially from some of the very small boys in first year. There was so many trying to have a go, it was difficult for me to get my boot in but I was proud to have done my bit. After a period of convalescence, George instantly became one of the nicest boys in the school and he actually became my friend despite me previously being terrified of him. Excellent education it was (my views only!).

Talking about body damage, I only had a few incidents but after one year at Hylands we moved to Dagenham as my father became the manager of a newsagent shop and even he thought that the local schools would be too tough for me. We decided that I would stay at Hylands and this meant that I would have to travel about 5 miles. Most days I would cycle to school after my paper round and on one occasion, I had a bit of an accident.

The road outside the school was named Park Crescent (It was a straight section of road ending in a cul-de-sac?) and was on a hill. One day I was tearing down this hill freewheeling when I looked down and noticed the front headlamp was vibrating out of its bracket when it suddenly fell off into the spokes of the front wheel. The bike stopped instantly and over I went flying through the air and landing on the gravel-surfaced tarmac. Palms and knees were impregnated with small stones and I still have some under the skin as a reminder of that day. This was my first knee damage but flying through the air was becoming a common occurrence.

I learnt that the way you fall and land is in direct relationship to the amount of pain you endure

My second knee damage occurred just before I left school when a big lump of a lad named Peter gave me such a bear hug that it squeezed all the wind out of me and caused me to fold up my legs just as he dropped me on my knees. You could hear the crunch of bone and he left me in much pain.

My school report is now quite comical to read with comments from my teachers such as 'Produced mainly rubbish' and for PE 'Rather ineffectual'. Those comments were designed to encourage me to do better?

One of the only females at the school was our music teacher. (The rumour was that she was a tank commander during the war!) One day during a singing lesson she finally discovered the source of the noise from a boy who was completely out of tune from the rest. She told me to stop singing and that I had to make sure that I never sung again. So I haven't.

When I was 15 years and three months, Mr Morgan the headmaster called me in and asked me if I wanted to leave school as he felt that I hated it and it would be better if I left. That was the best news I could ever have and I jumped at the offer. I left school at Easter 1965.

Chapter 10
Interests Outside Big Boys' School

Again, outside of school my life was full of interests and pleasure. These included collecting all sorts of things like stamps, cards and coins. I also started making model aeroplanes and carried on scouting (see next chapter). A further interest which was unusual was ship spotting. Yup, I know what you are thinking, this guy is a fully paid-up anorak.

Some Saturday mornings after completing my paper round I would either cycle or take a bus to Tilbury, Purfleet or Woolwich and check out each ship against my Ian Allen ship list books as they sailed past. The River Thames in those days was full of ships going to exotic places with ports of registration or flags only to be imagined. The little tugs and river barges, coasters carrying coal, oil, grain and timber every type of craft, I recorded it and observed them through my binoculars.

I would pay nine pence for the Tilbury ferry but it was free on the Woolwich ferry and I would try to ride on them all day until told to get off by the crew. I thought it was exciting until one day at school I confided in a pal what I got up to on a Saturday. He then told me that his dad was a tug captain. One day we cycled down to Woolwich where we waited in Royal Victoria Gardens next to the river. Chris told me that when his dad went past he would sound 'cock a doodle do' on his horn.

We waited and sure enough this old, tall, funnelled tug came up the river from London and sounded the horn. We frantically waved and the tug turned around in mid river and his dad came out of the wheelhouse and beckoned us to come down to the jetty next to the park. We left our bikes and ran down the gangplank to the pier. I thought I was in a dream, as we boarded the tug to be welcomed by the crew. We spent the day travelling up and down the Thames picking up and dropping off barges, seeing the huge thumping engine room and watching from the wheelhouse.

They dropped us off at Woolwich in the evening and we cycled home. What a day!

Chapter 11
Scouting for Boys

The motto of the Scouts is 'Be Prepared' and that is what I always try to be. My car is always packed with emergency tools and supplies for any eventuality. If you happen to have an accident and I am in the vicinity, I can supply a fire axe, bolt croppers, first aid, ropes, flame-proof gloves or anything else you may require to get out of a difficult situation. I have used them many times – although mainly on myself!

I became a cub scout when I was about eight years old and took to it like a duck to water. I continued to be a scout until I left school at 15. I loved every minute of it learning all sorts of skills and gaining the coveted badges. For some reason I was made a patrol leader (of the Peewit patrol) even though I was one of the smallest boys in the troop. We used to go camping in Thrift Wood Brentwood and Buckmore Park in Kent. We learnt useful things like how to light fires with two sticks and a bootlace, boil water in a paper bag and sing 'Ging gang goolie goolie goolie goolie watcha' round the camp fire with me miming of course.

One day at camp our scout leader arranged a 5-mile route march and decided that I should stay behind to do the washing and tidy up the camp. This was not a punishment as we all took turns at different tasks. Off they went and I got on with the washing. Once done, I needed a washing line fixed to some trees. I got the line fixed to one tree and pulled it across the camp to tie it to another tree. Being an 'excellent' tree climber, all I had to do was to climb up onto a tree and fix the other end of the line.

I was standing with one foot on a cut-off stump reaching up when my foot slipped and the stump run up my leg and hooked onto my shorts. There I was upside down hanging a few feet from the ground by my shorts and unable to extract myself. I tried many times to undo my shorts or hoist my way up but to no avail.

Just hanging around

As the troop marched into camp after many hours there, I was still hanging around looking exhausted and embarrassed. It took two scout leaders to unhook me. Later on I lay in my sleeping bag feeling sorry for myself with my cuts and grazes smeared in Germolene. The smell of Germolene still takes me back to that day. This never put me off scouting and I had many adventures with them, all of them exciting and interesting.

Chapter 12
Mugged

When I was about 13, I was fishing on my own at The Chase, which consisted of some old gravel pits a few miles from my home. After a few hours without a bite, I decided to change to the other side of the lake. As I walked along a path with all my fishing gear, I was pulled over from behind and punched in the face. I never saw my attacker and never knew why he did it as he did not steal anything from me. I staggered home and dad got the police involved but no one was caught.

Nowadays people get mugged all the time for many reasons such as robbery, racism, wearing the wrong clothes or just for the sheer fun of it. This is another reason why I started this book with the comment that I was born at the best possible time. Slowly, civilisation in this country and around the world has broken down and people do not respect each other. Have I been naïve to think that the years between 1945 and 1980 were safe, secure and civilised for the majority of the people and that now we are all at serious risk of being mugged, robbed, burgled and generally ripped off by – well, with the internet, it feels like most people in the world. We are not safe from our computers, our telephones and anyone who comes to our door or stops us in the street.

We are also living in a world where no one is to blame for their own accidents. It is always someone else's fault and then the claim lawyers come out of the woodwork and take them to court making both them and the person who had the accident lots of money. I often wonder where common sense and self-preservation has gone. Will it come to the point when we stay in bed all day for fear of someone harming us in some way?

The answer of course is to trust no one and tell everyone who contacts you about anything to leave you alone and go away.

Chapter 13
The Flower Show

Dad was well known for growing and showing flowers and he ended up judging at the Chelsea Flower Show and meeting the Queen. He grew mainly carnations in the garden and greenhouse and to get to this standard he would spend hours preparing the blooms for a show. There would be no baths on a Saturday evening if he had a show next morning, as all the blooms were laid out on racks in the bath. He used to take me over to the Dagenham Horticultural Society every Sunday on his bike. I used to sit on the crossbar and he usually came back with a smelly bag of manure on the back!

One day when I was about 8 years old he suggested that I should grow some blooms and put them in the Dagenham Town Show in the under 10-year-old section. He gave me half a dozen cuttings. The name was Frances Sellars and it was a medium red border carnation. I spent many hours nurturing these plants until they were producing lovely blooms.

On the day before the show I was very excited at the prospect of winning a prize. I read the entry form and it told me that the first prize would be rewarded with a silver cup, a red prize card and two shillings prize money. Were my blooms good enough to beat all the others? On the morning of the show I chose my best three blooms and dad and I went to the show. In the large marquee the tables were laid out and all the men were placing and arranging their pride and joy in each class. The junior class was in the far corner and I went over to prepare my blooms. I found a vase and arranged them in the middle of the table. They were all on their own and I could not understand why there were no other entrants. Perhaps they would turn up just before the judging. However, no one else turned up and the rest of the marquee was full to bursting, but the junior section was a bit forlorn with only my entry.

I was a bit smug that being the only entrant, I would walk away with the cup and prize money. We all left the marquee to allow judging to take place. After a few hours we were allowed back in and all the men started chatting and getting excited at their prizes. I went over to my entry expecting to see a red first prize card, only to find a blue SECOND prize card? What went wrong?

Dad was a bit surprised and went to speak to the judges and they told him that in their opinion, my blooms were not good enough for first prize even though there were no other entrants. It was another kick in the crutch for me and I have struggled to be interested in plants and gardening ever since. I also understood why they were having trouble getting any youngsters to be interested in flower growing!

Second out of one??

Chapter 14
Smog

Smog is smoke and fog mixed and because everyone burnt coal after the war, London often had smog in the autumn instead of fog. One day in 1963 I was at school in Hornchurch and living in Dagenham when the worst smog I have ever experienced came down. My mother phoned my school and asked if I could be told to make my way to my other grandparents' house about half a mile away.

The smog was a very thick yellow combination of water vapour and sulphur gas and it was difficult to even find the school gates. Once this was accomplished I went hand over hand using the garden fences as a guide along the roads. As I got to the end of each road, I bent down to make out the street name. When crossing the roads I firstly found the kerb then tried to imagine a 90-degree line across the road and walked in a straight line until the next kerb was found on the other side. Eventually, after some time I found my grandparents' house and knocked on the door.

I have got to say that my grandparents were always a bit strange but when the door was opened by my grandmother she demanded to know what I was doing on her doorstep. I explained that Mum told me to stay at her house tonight because of the smog and she was not happy. "Bob," she said, "Young Michael is here and he wants to stay the night." Granddad asked if I had eaten as they had already had their tea. I told them that I had a school dinner and was OK. I slept on the settee and went to sleep still hearing mutterings of complaint from my grandparents. I was certainly glad to get out and back to school in the morning.

Many years later my grandmother asked me to fix her television set as she thought the fuse had blown. After checking the fuse in the plug, I sat behind this large box of a TV with the back off, having unplugged it from the socket. Unbeknown to me the old televisions stored up masses amounts of electricity with all the valves and things inside. I sat on a low stool contemplating what bit to wriggle next and lent back when suddenly the stool gave way and I grabbed the bottom of the tele. A huge electric shock went through me as I struggled to regain my upright position on the stool. Even my teeth zizzed. Still fizzing and tingling with electric, I carefully replaced the back of the tele and told gran to get a repairman to look at it.

Fousands of volts fizzing through me

Chapter 15
My First Real Job

I left school on a Friday and started work at P G Woods & Sons the following Monday. I gave up working for my dad doing a paper round and I assumed this meant that I only had to work five days a week from now on instead of the seven days paper round. The company was just down the High Street in Dagenham, just a few minutes' walk away from where I lived.

P G Wood & Son was a small printing works with about half a dozen employees. My job was trainee/assistant compositor. They gave me a long white coat and £3 per week, with 10 shillings as tax and I gave10 shillings for my keep to my mum. This left me with £2 to spend. A compositor would make up the blocks of typeface that could then be fitted into a printing press to print all sorts of things. We printed letter headings, complement slips, business cards and wedding invitations, all the usual things. We also printed labels that were attached to bundles of newspapers which would indicate the starting train station, the time of the train etc. such as Euston to Paddock Wood via Waterloo, pick up 4.32am, delivery 5.56 am, collection by Joe Bloggs Newsagents etc. These changed daily and had to be printed last thing at night and had to be absolutely correct so a lot of unpaid overtime had to be worked.

It was hard work but at least they made me a box to stand on so I could reach all the different typeface boxes. I had to know them all and the different point sizes and spell it all correctly. I later found out that I am a bit dyslexic and wondered why I was so good at this job. However, I think that it must have been because I had to lay out the letters upside down and back to front.

Every Friday morning at exactly 10 o'clock I made the short journey in my dirty white coat from the works across the road to the bank while carrying a white cloth bag to collect the cash for the wages. After handing over the money requirements list, I would fill the bag with cash and walk back to the works. Why I was not mugged (again) was a miracle.

We worked in one large room with the printing presses only a few feet away from where we were compositing. When they were all printing, the noise was deafening with them crash crashing away. However, besides being dirty and noisy, I quite liked creating a block of typeface and seeing the completed documents.

I had the usual tricks played on me by the other members of staff like, go and buy a rubber hammer at the hardware shop. This was no problem as I had seen a motor mechanic called Stan who lived down the road using one and he got his from a garage shop, so I got one from there and told them to invoice P G Woods. The guys were very upset as they thought I would be laughed at in the hardware store and they meant to get me back.

One day after I had brought back the guys sandwiches from the bakery, I told one of them that he had not given me enough money and that he owed me another penny. Later on he came down the aisle and shouted, "Here's yer penny, you mean basket," and threw it to me. I caught it squarely in the palm of my hand and clasped it only for me to feel real pain and let it go. He had heated the coin up under the Ascot gas light holding it in a pair of pliers until it turned red and then threw it at me. I had Britannia burnt into the palm of my hand for a week. What a laugh they had!

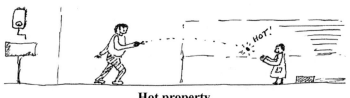

Hot property

After a year of very hard work with lots of unpaid overtime, I asked for a raise in pay only to be told that although I was becoming as good as my manager, I was too young to have any more pay and anyway, what was I doing with all my money to want more! I felt like Oliver Twist! I had to find another job if I wanted to get more money.

Chapter 16
The Start of My Construction Career

I was now 16 and I found a job as a drawing office trainee with a house builder in Romford. They were primarily estate agents but also built housing estates. They had a design office consisting of four surveyors and architects. It was like going into paradise, all very quiet, clean and light with intelligent refined people to work with. Totally unlike the noise of crashing printing machines, ink everywhere and uncouth men. They also had company cars, Mark 1 Ford Cortina's, my favourite car at the time.

On my first day the men in the office asked me my name and I told them they could call me Mike. That was no good as they already had a Mike in the office. "What's your middle name?" said Jim.

"Robert," I said.

"Right from now on you are Bob," so I answered to Bob for the next few years.

My starting pay was £5 per week but I had to travel to work on a bus which took away some of my money. The people were wonderful but as I had been to a boys' school and then in a man's world at the printing works, my knowledge of girls was very limited. The office had some female visions of loveliness which I could only admire from a distance as I was terrified of them. They would ask me to do some little job for them and I would gladly do as they wished.

Before getting the job, I had never answered a telephone and I was also terrified of the office phone. The other men realised this and made me answer it when it rang. To pick up this frightening instrument only to be told by Pam, one of the visions of loveliness on the other end, "Ah! Bob can you do me a little job?" would bring beads of sweat to run down my face – two terrifying things at once!

My first week was spent at an enormous drawing board and writing the letter 'A' with a drawing pen until it was perfect. Then I went onto letter B and so on until I could write the whole alphabet in upper and lower case. This was to ensure that the lettering on my drawings was to an architecturally acceptable standard.

As I had no qualifications, they sent me to college to take courses in surveying and building construction. I absolutely loved college as there were no bullies and the teachers actually wanted to teach! At work they taught me surveying, drawing and design. We set out roads and houses, carried out land surveys, inspected the builders' work whilst they constructed the houses and I had a wonderful time.

At the time, they were developing Hornchurch Airfield into a housing estate. This is where a few years before I had watched trainee RAF parachutists tumbling out of old barrage balloon baskets and gently floating down to earth. The lads were running out of designs for the houses so they asked me to design something new. We are not talking about anything architectural here, just the design of a box of rooms in different layouts and different elevations. Price £4900 for a house and £5100 with a garage.

Hornchurch Airfield Estate –
Unbelievably my designs are still standing!

One day we had a debate in the office about where to place the kitchen, should it be in the front of the house or the back. Some of the guys argued that the 'bored' housewife would prefer to look out of the front window so she could see all the goings on in the street and see the postman arrive etc. I argued that if she was looking out of the back window into the garden, she could see if her child had fallen into the fish pond...

Whilst at the company, I learnt to drive. Dad tried to teach me but after half an hour in his Hillman Imp he gave up and I went to the Cardrome Driving School with a proper driving instructor, Mr McNamara. As he instructed me he told me about all the horrific accidents that can befall a young driver including the one about not keeping a distance behind a lorry carrying telegraph poles and in a sudden stop, the pole went through the windscreen taking off the drivers head!

These stories induced me to learn quickly so that I would not have to listen to them so I ended up with only needing 12 lessons at 10/- (ten shillings – 50 pence) per hour. During my driving test I was driving down a quiet road with a few parked cars. Near one of the cars I slowed down and just as the examiner was about to ask why I had done so, a small boy walked out from behind the car in front on me. As I was only doing about 5mph, I stopped. He asked me how I knew the boy was there and I told him that I had seen his feet from underneath the car and I had assumed that he may well run out into the road. Even though I mucked up my reversing a bit and got a few questions wrong, he still passed me. I think it must have been because of that lucky boy.

I came home cock a hoop only for dad to tell me that in no way was I going to be allowed to drive his car as he was sure I was not up to proper driving. The company, however, had a Minivan which meant I could borrow it sometimes for work and on occasions at the weekend. After a few years at the company I asked for a pay rise but all they said was that I was too young to have any more pay and what was I doing with my money to want more anyway! I felt like Oliver Twist with the record stuck! I had to find yet another job to get more money.

Chapter 17
Peters & Barham Ltd

I found my next job at Peters & Barham, gravel producers with offices in South Street Romford. They had quarries all over Essex & Kent and I was employed as the assistant to the Estates Manager from 1968 to 1973, starting pay £8 per week. The Estates Manager was Jim an ex-coal mining surveyor from Yorkshire and a wonderful character. The managers and salesmen all smoked and drank heavily and most had additional women in tow. They worked very hard and played very, very hard. It was the making of me into a man, although I never smoked or had a second woman in tow.

Jim and I had to look after all the properties owned by the company which included houses, farms and the quarries themselves including all the processing plant. The job was so varied that I never got bored with the work.

By now dad had loaned me £200 to buy a 1960 Ford Poplar car and so I was mobile. I sometimes used this car for company business but often borrowed one of the company cars. One particular car was Jim's new white Ford Cortina Estate. A few weeks after it arrived, he came back one day with the back door smashed in. Someone had failed to stop when he stopped, so it went away for repair. A few weeks after it came back I was driving it in Chelmsford when a van with no brakes used me to stop and smashed the back door in…again.

It went away for repair and soon after it came back, Jim was driving it when someone smashed into the back again. So it went away for repair. Within a month after it was repaired again I was on the Embankment in London and stopped at a pedestrian crossing to let two girls cross. I heard a car coming up behind at high speed and looked in the rear view mirror and saw a Triumph TR4 sports car looming larger. I sounded my horn to alert the girls and pulled on the handbrake and stood on the brakes and waited for the crash…SMASH! I got out and a naval officer got out of his banana-shaped TR4 and demanded to know why I had stopped suddenly. Jim got rid of the jinxed Cortina soon after it came back from the repairers.

My 1960 Ford Poplar – I could not believe that someone stole my pride and joy one night. It must have been because of that 'go faster stripe'.

Chapter 18
Held Hostage

Peters & Barham was bought out by a Yorkshire company called Cawoods. They were also into sea-dredged gravel. This was dredged from the North Sea and brought into Bellamys Wharf in Rotherhithe South London. One of my jobs was to measure the hold of the ship before and after unloading so the volume of the cargo could be paid for. Often the ship would dock on the high tide in the middle of the night and I had to drive through Rotherhithe in the dark. In those days that area of London was rife with crime and the underworld. Luckily I never broke down and always locked my doors, but the thought was always with me on what would be my fate if I did (no mobile phones in those days). The job was dangerous enough, leaving the car on foot and then disappearing without a trace in South London.

Whilst the power station on the Isle of Grain in Kent was being built (now demolished), Cawoods had a jetty and a processing plant bringing in sea dredged gravel for the project. I had heard rumours that the men working on the jetty were upset because the company would not pay them any extra for working at night or weekends when a ship came in on the high tide. This was not my concern as I was only a surveyor.

One Friday morning Jim asked me that as I was going to Canterbury to carry out a survey, would I call into the Isle of Grain with the wages on my way down. "No probs Jim," I said. As I arrived onto the site, there was no one about; the place was deserted. I parked next to the site office and went in where I found all the men, about 8 of them. "Hi men, I've got your wages," and laid them out on the desk. "Everything OK?" I looked at the men and they did not seem to be very happy. The foreman grunted and I cheerily said, "Ah well I shall go then." The foreman said,

"Sit down sonny, you're not going nowhere."

"Don't be silly, I've got to do a survey at Canterbury and I'm late," and at that point I turned around to leave when a big bloke stood across the door.

"You are not going anywhere Mike, you're staying until we sort out this dispute." No matter how much I pleaded with them they were adamant that I was staying. "Sit there and phone your Jim, he's a good man, he'll understand," the foreman said.

And me hating the telephone!

Me: "Hi Jim, I am down at the Isle of Grain and am being held hostage, the men here want you to sort out their pay and conditions or else they will hold me until you do."

Jim: "Stop messing about Mike and get that survey done at Canterbury!"

Me: "Jim I'm serious, they won't let me go until you do…" He hung up!

Foreman: "Ring him again."

Me: "Jim it's me again, they are serious and won't let me go."

Jim: "Mike I'm not getting involved, go and do the survey…"

After convincing Jim they were actually serious, the day was spent with me negotiating their pay and conditions with the top man in Harrogate, Mr Binks the MD.

There were times of heated discussions between the men and the MD with me passing on the various colourful language down the phone. They did not want to talk to anyone except through me. It was hard work and emotional, no food, no tea, nothing, just talk.

Eventually, with me as a definite hostage, a ship full of gravel now stuck in the mud because by now the tide had gone out and the men getting very angry, the powers at be eventually gave in to their demands. So after 8 hours of being held hostage and negotiating my release I was finally able to drive home for tea. What an ordeal… negotiating an increase in money with a Yorkshireman.

Chapter 19
Site Investigation

One of my duties was to investigate new possible gravel quarries which meant digging holes in the ground. One day I was excavating holes in a field full of cows and the farmer had told me that they would leave us alone. The JCB dug some holes and I decided to leave some open to show Jim who would come to the site later.

As we were digging a hole, I casually looked over to one of the open holes and saw to my horror the whole herd surrounding it. As I started to walk over to shoo them away, one cow pushed another one into the hole! As I ran over to the hole, shooing the other cows away and swearing, I kept hoping that I was deluded. No such luck, there it was standing upright, 10 feet down a narrow slot in the ground making mooing noises.

Much running around to get the farmer, him swearing at me and then Jim turned up who also started swearing at me, me trying to persuade the digger driver to very carefully dig a ramp for the poor animal to walk out and trying to quieten down the farmer, whom I did explain to that he said they would be OK if we dug the holes!

Of course, just digging a ramp was not good enough because the cow had now got worried and had swelled up and was now not only 10 feet down but wedged tight. I told the farmer to go down the ramp and encourage his animal out and he retorted, "You effing well got it in there, you get it out!" So we dug another ramp at the other end for me to push it from the back, which worked but then I discovered that the worried animal had also relieved itself just where I was pushing, so now the cow was out and I was down a 10-foot hole and covered in…cow poo.

You go down – no, you go down…

Just after the cow and I came out of the hole, it caved in…

Chapter 20
Smoking and Ice Breaking

I have never smoked because I have tried to stay safe from all things that may harm me; however, I found that I did not need to do damaging things to my body on purpose because other events would take care of that.

Don Mingard was an elderly gentleman who helped out with our estates management. He was nearing retirement age and had commanded a fleet of bulldozers during the Battle of El Alamein. His troop had to take the bulldozers on low loaders past the enemy lines at night, doze out an airstrip so that as the Desert Rats pushed the Germans into retreat, they could immediately land the Hurricanes on them to re-arm and fuel. It was a heroic job which does not seem to be mentioned in the history books.

Don usually had two cigarettes on the go at any one time and lit up the next two with the butts. I spent a lot of time in the office unwittingly breathing in his smoke and sometimes I could not see him on the other side of a 10-foot office. His car was thick with tar, on the seats, the windows and the steering wheel. There was ash everywhere but he always offered his car to me for my use, which I accepted, reluctantly. One day after someone smashed into his car while I was driving it (it was a common occurrence) Don taught me a lesson which I have never forgotten. I walked into his office to break the news worried that he would get upset at the damage. He said, "Dear boy, forget the car; it's only a lump of metal not worth a jot, more importantly, are you all right?" Materiel things did not matter to Don.

We stayed one snowy February in the Mermaid Hotel in Rye as we were investigating the value of an existing gravel pit at Camber which was for sale, and was flooded with water. During the evenings in the pub over pints of beer, Don told me stories of his wartime desert experiences.

Don's job was to go through the gravel company's accounts in the site office and my job was to survey the surrounding land and the depths of water. I was provided with a small tug and an echo sounder. I set up marker poles around the quarry lake and we set off in the tug along straight lines across the water from one pole to the other. It was so frozen the tug had to break the ice with the captain trying to keep it on line while I sat at the back in the open, operating the echo sounder. I spent two days frozen to the bone, but what kept me going were the stories of the terrible hardship that Don and his men had ensured during the war. At least I was not under fire!

Frozen in time

Chapter 21
First Sight of My Guardian Angel

In 1971 the company bought me a mustard-coloured Mini complete with go faster wing mirrors. It had a new-fangled accessory that had just appeared on new cars in the form of seat belts. These hung from the door pillar and had to be adjusted manually as inertia belts had not been invented. I never used them as only a wimp of the first order would be seen with them on. There they hung unused, getting in the way of surveying instruments and girl activity.

One day I was coming back from a survey whizzing up Noak Hill near Brentwood when a Triumph 2000 came out of a turning right in front of me. I was doing about 40 mph and I realised I was going to hit him broadside. I remember thinking that perhaps I should have worked out how to use the seat belts when SMASH! We careered across the road and we both hit a telephone box. As the steam from my radiator died down, I went to get out of my mangled Mini and looked down to see my seat belt on, fully adjusted. I had to find out how to undo the belt as I had never used it before.

How did my seat belt become adjusted and fixed across me? I have no idea except that my guardian angel may have known how to fix it! The man in the Triumph was OK and saying how lucky I was to have worn my seat belt because he never did – no one ever did! It was not until 1983 when the wearing of seat belts became compulsory, but I have always worn mine ever since that crash.

My lovely Mini before the crash

Chapter 22
The Tiger Moth

You should know by now that I am an anorak because I am interested in most things and always need something to do with my spare time. My 'enormous' pay packets from P G Wood and Cawoods meant that I could indulge in hobbies that cost money such as building and flying model aeroplanes. These constructions took up not only my time but part of the conservatory at my parents' house, testing my mother's patience.

The damage that I caused to myself is untold because the use of razor blades, pins, glue, dope and fuel including nitro methane, not to mention spinning propellers. All these had an effect on my body that other hobbies cannot possibly do. The first aid kit was in constant use and one piece of glass from the top of a pin remained in my thumb for about 20 years until it came out one morning on its own accord.

I would spend hours building them only for my pride and joy to crash at our flying ground at Central Park, Dagenham. One such model was of a Tiger Moth. I finished it in the colours of a Super Tiger known as The Canon. There were three of them, The Bishop, The Deacon and The Canon. The model flew very well until one day a strong gust of wind caught it which caused it to spin in and crash.

My model of The Canon

The next year, 1969, I decided to have a week's gliding course at Challock Lees near Canterbury. This was my second year with the Kent Gliding Club where I went for one week and had intensive flying lessons on a Slingsby T21 glider which flew not much better than a brick. We were towed up into the air on a long tow line and at about 1000 feet we released it and it took just a few minutes for us to do a circuit and land.

Me examining the flying brick with my instructor

This particular year a Tiger Moth flew in to give aero tows to the club members who flew proper gliders. It would take them up to about 3000 feet and let them go. I was amazed when I realised that the Tiger was in fact 'The Canon'.

The real Canon at Challock Lees

It was Wednesday evening and the club members were being towed by the Tiger. We had tidied all the bricks away in the hanger and were queuing to get our dinner in the club house when we heard the Tiger doing a low pass over the field to drop his tow rope as he was finished for the evening. As the rope dropped to the ground, the engine stopped dead and it all went quiet. He was heading for the escarpment of the North Downs and we were all told by the instructors that if you were in this position, to glide out across the downs and find a field to land in – never turn around as you may well stall and crash.

What did the pilot do? He tried to turn around to land back on the airfield, but as he turned the Tiger stalled and spun straight in. Everyone stared in horror, dinner plates crashed to the floor and people gasped. They were all frozen to the spot, except one prat – me. I rushed to the French windows, opened them and ran (in my slippers) towards the crash. As I was running, the thought occurred to me that I may see something I may not like.

The pilot was unconscious with his face covered in blood as he had hit the instrument panel, but as I looked at him my instructor came running up and shouted at me to get the fire extinguisher from the control caravan. I ran as fast as I could and came back with it as the instructor pulled at the framework with his hands. Eventually, the ambulance came and took the poor chap away. He had broken his back but after six months he was back flying again. Sadly, the Tiger was never repaired.

Looks the same as my model – after it crashed

Chapter 23
The Boat

The managing director of Cawoods wanted to sell his sailing dinghy. It sat in one of the workshops and I mentioned it to Dad who suddenly said, "I'll buy it!" He paid £100 for it together with a trailer. We picked it up, hitched to his Ford Zodiac and found that he had bought a very nice boat. We had an awful lot of fun taking it down to St Lawrence bay near Hullbridge and sailing it all day. It was a very safe and stable boat until one day we hit a wreck and it started to sink. I jumped out with a rope attached and swam ashore pulling it into shallow water.

Captain Haddock at the tiller

One Friday evening my friend Gary and I were at the Ilford Palais night club when we just about pulled a couple of girls. We brought them some drinks and had a few dances (well, not dances – sort of shuffle about). Whilst chatting them up I mentioned that I had my own yacht and would they like to come aboard. "Yes," they said, "shall we say this Sunday?" After getting their addresses, we arranged to pick them up Sunday morning with a comment from us to 'bring your bikinis!'

After begging Dad to not only borrow the boat but also his Zodiac to tow it, I picked up Gary and then we went around the girl's houses to pick them up. I think they were a bit taken aback by the fact that our 'Yacht' was actually small enough to be towed behind a car, but the day was hot and sunny and all was smiles. Gary and I looked at each other – *We've cracked it*, we thought.

We went to Two Tree Island near Leigh on Sea as they had a public slipway into the sea channel. The channel was full of every sort of boat and ours looked a bit small in comparison. However, we launched and sailed down the channel into the Thames up to Southend. It was a hot day and soon the girls took off their clothes to reveal their bikinis. Gary and I did the same and revealed our scrawny white bodies clad in our swimming trunks (not woollen ones). We sailed around for ages taking turns at steering, tacking and other nautical things. After some time we thought that it would be a good idea if we headed back and noticed that most of the other boats had already gone.

We sailed into the channel leading back to the slipway and found that the tide had gone out and the water in the channel was very much narrower than before. There were large areas of oozy black mud on both sides. As we got closer to the launch slipway, the keel board scraped the bottom, so we pulled it up and reduced the sail. We were still about quarter of a mile from the slipway when the water really ran out and we were stuck in the mud. The only thing we could do was for Gary and I to get out into the mud and drag the boat back. The girls at this stage had lost all of their giggles and were becoming a bit fractious.

We dragged the boat slowly along getting covered in black mud until the point when we were about 100 yards from the slipway and at this point we could drag it no more. "I'm afraid that you two girls will have to get out and help us," I said.

"OMG! You are joking?" Out they climbed into the deepest ooze in their bikinis and pulled and pushed. As we arrived at the slipway, the old local sea dogs were waiting and laughing, they could not contain themselves seeing four semi-naked youngsters covered from head to foot in poo.

For some reason we never saw the girls again – I don't think they had a taste for adventure?

"I'm afraid that you two girls will have to get out and help us."

Chapter 24
Fishing

One of my other hobbies was fishing and this was mostly an incident-free sport. How could anything go wrong besides falling in the water which I did a few times or getting mugged, but nothing unusual to tell you until the day I decided to go to a local lake with my future wife Gill, my mate Barry and his new girlfriend, Maggie. The girls were a bit bored and were lying on the grass bank, some way back from the water. Barry and I were casting our lines into the lake, sometimes catching the line in a tree and having no luck with any fish.

As Barry swung his rod forward to cast another line, it whipped backwards and the reel went – gizzzzzz! Then came a *SCREEEEAM!* from behind. We both turned around and saw Maggie clutching her face. The fishhook had caught in her eyelid and as Barry went forward he threw down the rod which only pulled the line tighter. Oh! The fuss and bother we had getting it out, how much can a girl panic? I seem to have made things worse by saying "Hold still while I get this pesky wriggling maggot off the hook!" A few years later they got married and I bet she insisted that Barry gave up fishing.

Oh! The fun of catching something

Chapter 25
The White Jumper

My days of being bullied came to an end one Saturday evening in 1967 outside the Chequers Public House. I had gone out for the evening which included having a few drinks in the pub even though I was, at the time, under age by a few months. My mother had asked me if I would befriend a new lad in the district called John whose mother had said he did not have any friends.

John turned out to be a bit wayward and my friends and I suffered his moods for quite a few months until that Saturday evening. He had turned up in a new white roll neck jumper which his mother had knitted and was going on about how good he looked.

After a few drinks, he started to get rough with some of my mates and I told him to stop. He turned on me and said, "Come outside and I'll sort you out."

And I said (after having a few drinks myself), "Come on then, let's have it out." We both went outside into the car park.

Bucket (Mr Powell, my PE teacher) had shouted at his victims, "DON'T SEND ME A TELEGRAM SO I CAN SEE YOUR PUNCH COMING, JAB ME IN THE FACE!" He explained that your nose is very weak and even a light jab will usually stop most people in their tracks. That advice had registered with me and it all came back in that dark car park.

Don't send him a telegram!

A small crowd surrounded us and I was in the imaginary ring with John who was telling me how he was going to pulverise me. Suddenly he came at me raising his fist behind his head to get in a good punch – he had sent me a telegram! As he closed in I suddenly jabbed my fist towards his nose and the effect was unbelievable. He fell backwards and his nose started to bleed – all down his new white jumper. I think it must have been the first time someone had beaten him in a fight. He was distraught that the jumper was now covered in red. After that day I vowed that no one would ever bully me again because I now had a secret weapon – and no one ever has.

Chapter 26
Snared

Have you been in one of those situations where at first it seems minor and then it becomes a bit more serious. For instance, you lock yourself out of the house and you think 'Oh bother' and then you realise that you have left the oven on or something and then you think, 'Ah! I shall have to smash the window' and then you think 'Well that will set off the alarm to the police station and they will think I'm a burglar'…you know what I mean.

Well, around 1971 I was doing a field survey at a place called Newney Green near Chelmsford and we were putting in a planning application for a new quarry. I needed to check what crops were in each field for compensation purposes. So, on a nice sunny day, I set off across the fields with my maps and was in the middle of nowhere with the skylarks singing when I came across a wide, deep ditch with steep banks. I had no hesitation in jumping the crevasse but I only made it halfway up the far bank. As I leapt up the bank I was pulled back by something attached to my ankle.

I lay up the bank in the grass and looked down to see that I had landed in a wire snare which was tightly wrapped around my ankle. At first I thought all I had to do was to loosen it and be on my way, but as I bent down, I found that the sliding connector that made the wire loop was a one-way ratchet affair. However much I tried I could not slide it loose.

I thought the next thing would be to pull out the stake holding the wire snare. This turned out to be a length of steel driven deeply into the ground. It would not budge. So there I was laying unseen in a deep ditch, miles from any road or building with no hope of anyone passing nearby any time soon. I then realised that I had not told anyone what I was doing and had not even seen the farmer before I started. No one would find me until the man came to check the snare!

One foot either way and I would have missed it

I lay on the bank kicking the stake with the sole of my free foot working it loose, stopping every now and again for a breather. Every kick I gave it I cursed the person who would put up such a horrible trap.

Eventually, I managed to pull the stake out of the ground and I got to the top of the ditch so that I could sit there in more comfort to wriggle loose the ratchet. All this took me about two hours and I finally sat there with a cut around my ankle and this horrid thing in my hand. I stood up and threw the contraption as far into the field as I could muster. I hobbled back to my car and decided that the survey could be carried out on another day.

Chapter 27
The Bullnose

The company had gained planning permission to open up a new quarry in Asheldham on the Dengie Peninsula in Essex. This is a remote area of land midway up the coast between Southend and Colchester. The land was owned by a very old farmer who looked a bit like Fagin from Oliver Twist. He had bought a nice bungalow in the village to retire to because his house was to be demolished as part of the quarry.

One day I had to visit him to make sure that he was alright and if he needed any help with moving and was accompanied by our production manager, Tommy Farr. He was in charge of all the quarries and was a big cheese in the company. (He was also a big character and drank, smoked and womanised excessively). The old farmer opened the door and asked us if we wanted a cup of tea and we reluctantly said yes. The kitchen was something to be avoided at all costs but we had to be seen to be sociable.

We asked him if we could do anything for him and he said that he needed to get rid of some large furniture that he could not move and Tommy offered to get rid of it for him and said that he might be able to get some money for it to give to him. "Anything else you need to get rid of?" I asked.

"Ah, now I have got to sell my car which is in the garage, I haven't driven it for some time and I don't think it can be worth much, come and see what you think."

We went out to a tumble down garage and he opened the doors and there it stood, a 1926 Bullnose Morris in yellow with red leather seats and black trim, covered in bird poo.

A similar Bullnose but without the bird poo

The old man said, "I haven't driven it since the war started because petrol was on ration, do you think it is worth anything?" and I stared at it. It was perfect except for the bird poo and I said, "I'll offer you £100 for it."

"Oh, I couldn't take that much for it Mike, you have been so helpful to me," he said.

"No. I insist," I said. "Can I pick it up on Saturday?" So the deal was done and I went home to tell Dad all about it. He offered to lend me the money and it would be a great restoration project. I could not wait.

Saturday came and Dad and I went down to pick up the Bullnose. I knocked on the door and the old man opened it and looked surprised to see me. "Hallo, I've come to pick up the car."

He looked puzzled and said, "The other man came early today and took it away, I thought you were buying it together." I could not believe my ears. Tommy presumably sold it on straightaway as he was not the sort of man who would want a car like that. When I tackled him about it, all he said was, "First come first served, tough luck." Nice.

However, I recently found out that he survived a Japanese prisoner of war camp during the war and for that I can forgive him anything.

Chapter 28
An Electrifying Change of Job

By 1973 I longed to start getting a good wage so I had to change my job again. Cawoods was a great job but the pay was only £600 per year and I wanted £1000! I was either greedy or ambitious. I was eventually poached by an earthmoving contractor based in Essex. They removed all the clay soil from Cawoods quarries to expose the gravel, so I knew the company and they knew me. They not only offered £900 per year but also a yearly bonus and a bright yellow Ford Cortina Mk3! I thought I was now on my way up!

Daytona yellow Cortina – the bees knees

This job also produced a number of great adventures over the next 28 years during my time with them. The first one occurred soon after I started when my new boss got a phone call from my old boss to ask if I could help out with a post earthmoving survey that was being carried out by one of our competitors. My boss Ian asked me to go to a quarry near Chelmsford and meet Cawoods new surveyor Norman and the contractor's surveyor, David. We met up in the site office and we then drove down to the quarry.

I was nominated by the two of them to read the survey instrument, Norman would hold the staff and David would write down my readings, so the three of us donned wellie boots and started work. Things were going well and suddenly black clouds came over and it started to rumble with thunder with a bit of lightning in the distance. Norman came over and said, "I think we should pack up, that storm looks bad and I'm holding a metal staff." David and I looked at each other and thought, *What a wimp*. I told Norman that we would finish the survey in ten minutes and that as it wasn't raining and we were 30 feet down a hole in the ground, the chances of being struck by lightning was nil. Norman walked back to the face of the quarry and turned around and I looked through the instrument and was adjusting the focus when – FLASH BANG! Something whacked me over the head with a sledgehammer and it all went black.

I awoke and I was lying on the ground soaked to the skin; it was pouring with rain and David was lying nearby unconscious. I got him up on his feet and we collected up our gear. The metal staff was lying where we last saw Norman but he was nowhere to be seen. Both suffering a headache, we trudged up the slope out of the quarry.

We eventually came back to the site office and went in where we found poor Norman standing in the corner shaking from head to foot. He could not believe it when we walked in soaked to the skin and looking like death but slightly warmed up. Apparently, he watched in horror as the lightning bolt struck the instrument and obviously went through my eyeball down my body and the charge came off my elbow and hit David standing next to me. We both went down looking very dead and then it immediately started to pour with rain.

I asked him if he had called an ambulance and he quivered that he did not see any point as he thought we were dead. If it had not been for the fact that we were both wearing rubber wellington boots and were not wet with rain, we certainly would have been.

Flash, bang, wallop!

Now was Norman a wimp? Probably not, he was in fact very intelligent and had a lot of common sense. We, on the other hand…?

Chapter 29
Honeymoon Bliss

Gill and I were married in January 1974 and it was freezing cold
– well it would be in the middle of winter! After spending our
first honeymoon night in our tiny terraced house in Brentwood,
we travelled to the Cotswolds the next day. As we arrived on the
outskirts of Oxford, my yellow Cortina gave a jolt which I
though was a bit strange but the engine kept running so we
carried on.

We arrived at our destination, an old public house in
Langford (you know, the village between Broughton Poggs and
Filkins??) which had been recommended by Mr Mingard (of
Desert Rat fame). He had let the landlord know that we were
coming and as we entered the pub and all the yokel locals said
congratulations with a wink. We were romantically shown to our
freezing cold room with a one bar electric fire and twin beds…
some honeymoon!

Next day, the car would not start so the landlord called a
local mechanic who found that the points within the distributor
(the whirly thing which makes the engine fire and go – for the
non-mechanical readers) had snapped and at the same time
welded themselves together to keep the spark going with the
broken bits until I turned off the engine. "My God, I've never
seen anything like this before," said the mechanic. "You were
really lucky as it should have stopped dead." I was not totally
sure of that statement that we were lucky as a night in Oxford
may have been better and warmer and we may even have had a
double bed.

The next day I contracted really bad flu and we had to cut
the honeymoon short. I had to drive home with me feeling
shivery and weak but the best bit was that Gill had phoned her
sister and mother and they welcomed us with a warm house and
a supper of hot stew.

Chapter 30
Trying to Run Over a Policemen

I used the Rotherhithe tunnel on quite a few occasions. This tunnel is very narrow as it was built in the mid nineteenth century for horse and carts. It has steep entry roads at either end running into the tunnel entrance. One very sunny day in 1975, I was coming down the entrance road with the bright sun in my eyes and suddenly saw some feet walking about in the middle of the road. I braked hard but I knew I was going to hit the person. However, the apparition jumped out of the way just in time and he banged on the side window as I passed him and I realised it was a policeman.

I had stopped about 10 yards past him and he came running up and pulled open the door. Then he grabbed me by the collar to drag me out but nearly strangled me with the seat belt. He was shouting at me, "What the eff are you doing, you nearly effing well run me over you little effing squirt, take that belt off, so I can effing well sort you out… etc." I undid my seat belt and as he dragged me out my foot came off the brake (I had not had a chance to pull the handbrake on) and as he started on me again, the car slowly rolled down the hill towards the tunnel. "You effing little… Argg! Get back in there and stop that effing car rolling." I caught it up and jumped in to pull on the handbrake.

As I looked back the policeman was stopping cars further up the ramp and then came back to me, by now he had calmed down a bit. "Did you not see I was trying to stop you? We've had an accident in the tunnel, you effing little toe rag! I could book you for something if I could think of what it would be." He was still shaking. I thought he was quite lucky actually.

When my mother proofread this book she said, "I think you have put too many 'effs' in the story, dear." I had to tell her that I had actually taken most of them out!

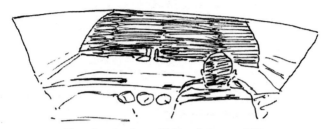

Two feet in the middle of the road??

Chapter 31
Drunk in Charge

Drink driving laws came into force in 1974 but was not really considered a proper offence until 1980. This means that the average person took no notice of them and I am not proud to say that I was one of them. Strangely I actually thought that I was a better driver when I was a bit tiddly. I wonder why?

I carried out a survey of a quarry in 1978 with Stewart, the new surveyor of Cawoods. We had removed all the overburden from the gravel and had to calculate how much earth we had moved and therefore how much Cawoods owed us for the work. We usually did the surveys in the morning and retired to a local pub at lunchtime. We then worked out the quantity of earth moved and how much it cost, had a few beers and lunch, shook on the deal and went back to our offices.

As an aside, the calculation for the money had to be derived from working out the cubic yards of earth moved using survey levels in feet and decimal feet. Then if the cost per cubic yard was eleven pence half penny, this had to be multiplied by the number of yards and converted into pounds and pence. It required us to have lots of zeros in our calculations and all this was carried out long hand as we did not have any calculators in those days. We then both worked out the money independently and often came to a figure within a few pennies.

On this particular day we did the survey at Newney Green quarry (remember the snare incident and the lightning? This quarry had a jinks on me.) After the survey we went to the Duck public house in the village. We had lunch and did our calculations together with a few beers and was about to leave when some other managers from Cawoods came in. Could they buy us a drink, they said. Of course we accepted. So we stayed…and then the landlord said, "Time to close up!"

And we said, "Oh! Do we have to go?"

And he said, "Well, I shall lock the doors and you can keep drinking if you want to…" so we stayed…until opening time at 6 o'clock.

When we left, Stewart could not stand (for some reason?) and I said, "You can't drive home in that condition, leave your car here and I will take you." So we all helped him to my car and I drove him home to Chelmsford and then I made my way back to Braintree. Apparently (according to my wife Gill) when she came back from the stables, she found a shoe near the back door, followed by a sock, followed by a pair of trousers followed by a trail of my remaining clothing up the stairs. I was fast asleep in bed…obliviously happy.

Chapter 32
Late for Tea Again

In 1977 my boss Ian and I drove down through the Dartford Tunnel to look at a proposed site now called Crossways Business Park. At the time the area was just a large area of marshland and the proposal was to bring in sea-dredged gravel and fill the area up and then build on it. The huge Littlebrook D power station was also being built by John Laing Construction at that time.

It was difficult to see the area of marshland, so Ian suggested that we find a way onto the sea wall. I drove along a lane and found another track which seemed to go towards the River Thames. "Go that way," said Ian and off we went. He was right and we ended up at a ramp which went up onto the seawall. When we got up there, it was quite a good track and we drove for about two miles along it towards the power station following the river with the ships going past.

As we went round a bend, there was a puddle in front of us which went on for about 20 yards. "Hum," I said, "that looks a bit deep Ian, get out and see if it is." Out he got and walked around it.

"It's fine, Mike, come on." As I drove forward, the wheels started to spin and eventually, I got well and truly stuck. Ian and I tried to put all sorts of bits of driftwood under the wheels but all that happened was the car sunk deeper into the mud. What to do?

Ian then had a brainwave. He knew people at the power station site and we may be able to borrow a Land Rover to pull us out, so we trudged along the sea wall to the site compound about a half a mile away. As we walked into the site, we noticed a Land Rover in a compound. It was not John Laing but an electrical contractor called Holliday Hall Ltd. We knocked on the door of the site office and walked in. There was a young man about 30 playing darts with a young woman about 25. Ian asked

92

if we could borrow the Land Rover and after explaining why, the man told us that he would have to drive it as we would not be insured and secondly he could not spend long on the operation because he had a dinner date with his new wife and could not be late.

It was obvious that he had never driven a Land Rover before because the first thing he did was to look for the choke button to start the engine. I suggested that it may be a diesel, so it would not have a choke. He did not listen and proceeded to pull at each knob. Eventually, he grabbed the windscreen wiper knob and pulled – hard – the whole dashboard pulled away from the frame with a plastic crunching noise and he blasphemed a bit. I again suggested he should just turn the key and when he did, it started. Off we went along the track and onto the sea wall. I suggested to him that he should turn around and reverse along the sea wall and then he could pull us forwards. His reversing was… a bit wobbly and he nearly put us over the wall on a number of occasions.

We eventually got to my car and he slowly reversed towards the puddle. I told him to only put his rear wheels into the mud and to keep the front wheels on the dry ground so he could get a good grip with the front wheels. As I attached the rope between the two vehicles, I noticed two men running across the marsh towards us waving something…a bit strange? Anyway, as we asked him to drive forward, he had still got it in reverse gear and he went backwards into the puddle and sunk into the mire. Oh dear, still, the four-wheel drive should pull us out. He then had trouble getting it into four-wheel drive, so I jumped into the driver's seat and took over. I put it in four-wheel drive just as two panting mechanics arrived from the marsh holding a…front prop shaft!

Through the barrage of swear words I managed to understand that they had been in the middle of changing the prop shaft and had taken it to be repaired and when they got back the Land Rover had disappeared. I then tried to drive it out of the mud in two-wheel drive and guess what – we were now both stuck! Of course, the mechanics could not fit the prop shaft because the Landy was deep in doo-doo. They then saw the smashed dashboard and they went berserk! By this time the ships in the Thames had their lights on as it started to get dark. The young man who was only trying to help us was now covered in mud (because as I spun the wheels, he got in the way and the mud covered him from head to foot), he had been verbally abused by the mechanics and was now very late for his dinner date. He walked back along the sea wall with the calls from the mechanics like, "Yeah, that's right, you walk away from it and leave us to sort it out!"

Ian walked back with him to get another vehicle from John Laing to pull us both out and came back with a four-wheel drive forklift truck. In the pitch dark, as the lighted ships sailed past, the mechanics got their Land Rover back and Ian and I got off the sea wall and made our way back to Essex. I often wondered what trouble the young man got into with his new wife and also if he ever offered to help anybody ever again.

**We watched the ships go past in the river
with their lights on**

Chapter 33
Food Poisoning

I would imagine that everyone has had food poisoning at one time or another and I have had it bad a few times. The first time, however, was the worst and it happened on a Saturday in 1975 when I took Gill to Epping shopping whilst I went into work at my office. After work I picked her up and we drove down to a pub in a local village for lunch. We both had cottage pie and then travelled home. As we arrived, Gill started to feel sick and rushed into the house. I felt fine though.

On the following Tuesday, we were on holiday and we drove to my parents' house in Dagenham but as I pulled up, I started to feel unwell. I got into the house and ran to the loo where I successively had sickness and the runs. After a while my mother and Gill were outside the loo door asking me if I was alright and I managed to open it. I was exhausted. The worst bit then started – I sat back on the loo and clear water started to run out of me like a tap which I could not turn off. My body fluids had decided to vacate me and I was getting worse. Gill & mother then laid me on a bed and called a doctor who examined me and suggested I had food poisoning and that I should recover quickly, but as he got up to go, I started to convulse. He called for an ambulance and I was rushed to Hackney Isolation Hospital with the blue lights flashing. During the journey they strapped me down on a stretcher but I got my arms free so that I could put my fingers down my throat to be sick and at the same time my tap was still running water.

They thought that I had contracted some deadly disease such as Lassa Fever which is caught in West Africa from animals and they did not believe Gill when she told them I had not been abroad recently. "I think I would have known if my husband had gone to Africa!" demanded Gill. They gave me a lumbar puncture in my spine by placing a towel in my mouth so I could not scream and then took me to an isolation room and fed drips into me. The doctors reckoned that I would have been dead in another few hours' if my fluids had not been replaced.

On about the third day of lying in my lonely bed a nurse reset the drip in my arm. Unfortunately, she did not hit a vein and a few hours later I was in agony with my arm swelling up. By now it was nighttime, so I rang for the night nurse and explained that I was in much pain. She shrugged it off and told me to accept it. I lay awake all night and to take my mind off the pain. I studied my wristwatch and concentrated on the hands slowly going round. In the morning a new nurse came in and she took one look at my arm which was now swollen and bright red and pulled the drip out.

After a week of lying in my isolation room I was suddenly told to leave the hospital as they needed my bed. Because I had no phone or money to contact someone to pick me up I had to sit on the hospital steps in my pyjamas for four hours until collected by my sister-in-law. It took another six months for me to get back to normal. We all decided that it was the cottage pie that caused the food poisoning because Gill was sick soon after she ate it whereas the bugs stayed with me for days to multiply. It was a close call because if I had not convulsed in front of the doctor, I may not have got to hospital in time.

**Sitting on the steps of the Isolation Hospital
in my pyjamas**

I had another bout of food poisoning recently, not as bad as the one above but not nice. I decided to take Gill for a birthday treat to a really posh hotel in London. The day before we went I was working at a site in Dagenham and one of the guys came into the office and said, "Anyone want a bacon roll, we had too many made for the meeting?" Feeling a bit hungry, I took one and I think this was the cause of my suffering.

We turned up at the posh hotel next day and we were given a really good room. We changed and went into Piccadilly and into the Burlington Arcade looking at things that we could never afford and then had a lovely meal at an excellent restaurant. We went to bed and fell asleep. At midnight I woke up and felt a bit sickly. After being sick from both ends I came back to bed. Then at 1 am I repeated the performance and then at 2 pm, then at 3 pm and by 4 pm I was laying on the cold floor of the bathroom, out of it. After another hour, I climbed back into bed covered in sick and wrapped in my dressing gown, shivering.

In the morning when Gill woke up, she saw a smelly white form lying in bed, croaking, "Happy Birthday, Gill." We decided that we should go home and leave the hotel to clear up the mess. After sorting out our cancellation at reception, Gill found the cleaner and told her what had happened and what she may find in the bathroom and the lady said,

"Oh! Not to worry, we have lots of blue liquid that will sort that out!!" She hadn't at that point seen the devastation. We came home by taxi. My unfortunate wife Gill has had a number of birthdays disrupted caused by me being within her vicinity!

Chapter 34
Building the M25 Motorway

In 1979 my company won the contract to carry out the earthworks on a section of the M25 from Aveley to the Dartford Tunnel. It was February and very cold when we set foot on site for the first time. As we banged the first peg into the ground, the consulting engineer with us said, "I hereby announce that this road is from today, outdated." He explained that it should have four lanes on both sides to cope with the predicted traffic but they were told by the government that they had to cut costs and build it with only three lanes each side. 34 years later after many traffic jams, it has finally been widened.

During the construction, I experienced many incidents which may interest the reader. My first story is about a site portacabin which was located in the centre of the A13 roundabout and a labourer was asked to collect up a lot of waste timber and get rid of it. He decided to set fire to it but the wind kept blowing out the matches, so he piled them up against the portacabin and it soon caught fire – the wood and the cabin. I had just driven up when I saw the flames and rushed into the cabin to get everyone out. We stood back watching the cabin go up when the gas cylinder suddenly blew up and it went roaring across the roundabout skimming the bonnet of a car, which then nearly crashed into the barrier around the verge with the other cars swerving all over the place trying to miss him.

Good shot!

Another labourer came to me one day and asked if he could have a redundant manhole cover. I thought he wanted it for scrap, so I told him that he could. Later on I stopped and asked him why he wanted it and he proudly said that he collected them and this one had a nice pattern on it. As I collected things when I was young, it seemed reasonable that he had a nice interest in things, but I had to ask him some more questions as it seemed an unusual hobby.

Q1. "Where do you keep them?"
Ans. "In my bedroom."
Q2. "How many have you got?"
Ans. "Oh, about ten now."
Q3. "Ten covers would be very heavy, do you think the floor joists in your bedroom would be able to take that sort of weight?"
Ans. "It's a council house which is very strong so it should be OK."
Q3. "Where you get the other covers from?"
Ans. "I got them from the road at night. If I see a nice one I just pull them up and roll them home!"

Presumably, leaving holes in the road for people and cars to fall down!! I explained to him that I did not think this was a very good idea and suggested that he took brass rubbings of them instead. I gave up explaining about brass rubbings to him after a bit, as I think he thought I was balmy.

Talking about scrap metal, we had two large redundant cast iron gas pipes under a road that had to come out. We had to excavate the road for a new bridge and these two redundant pipes had to be disposed off site. It becomes the contractor's responsibility to dispose of all waste which includes scrap metal.

Pre 1990 this scrap was always considered a perk for the men and the company turned a blind eye to the sale of it. One Friday, Ken, my foreman, came to me and asked that if he and a few men could work over the weekend, they could dig out the pipes and get rid of them so we could carry on excavating the earth the next week and asked if he could he have my permission to do it. I told him that he could but I did not want to know what would happen to the scrap iron. I duly forgot about it.

I drove onto the site on Monday morning and it was bucketing with rain. As I stopped, the doors of my Land Rover opened and in jumped Ken and two other men with a carrier bag. Ken shoved the wet bag into my lap and said, "This is what we got for the scrap iron and we want you to share it out as you are good at arithmetic; there's £750 in there." (That was a lot of money in those days.) I was dumbfounded as I have never got involved in this sort of thing before and a further shock came when I said,

"Split into three is £250 each."

"No," said Ken, "even we could do that sum, no we want you to share it, so divide it by four." Suddenly, I was not only guilty of allowing the men to work over the weekend on their own but I was now party to gaining money, not totally legally.

A week later I was in my site office having a meeting with my boss and managing director when the door burst open and a driver who had been on holiday over the past two weeks stood there. I turned and said, "Doug, I am in a meeting as you can see, can you come back later?" He was in a rage and shouted

"That was my scrap iron, and you and Ken stole it from me, I was looking forward to having that, you stole it off me, I want my money!!" I must have gone scarlet and rushed out of the office to calm him down and sent him away. As I walked back into the office, dreading what my MD would say, he just said,

"The men are like children sometimes Mike, and he is particularly greedy. I am glad he did not get anything this time, say no more about it." And that was that, no more was said but it was an incident that I did not enjoy.

Chapter 35
The Pack of Hounds

My company also won the second stage of the M25 which went up through Belhus Park Aveley and on towards Upminster. It cut through a large area of land owned by a gypsy and he kept about a hundred horses on it. One day we found a dead horse within the line of the new road. Harry, my head supervisor, offered to take me to his yard to tell him. We pulled up at a five-bar gate and beyond lay his yard with his caravan on the far side. A barn was over to the right and all looked peaceful. Harry said, "We don't both have to go, you go and I'll wait here in the car."

I opened the gate and went in and started to walk across the yard towards the caravan. When I was halfway across I heard the barking of dogs as two Rottweilers and two Jack Russells came storming out of the barn towards me snarling and barking in full flight. I went cold and stuck my hands into my pockets and kept walking. As they crashed into me I started talking calmly to them and saying what good dogs there were etc.

I felt like a fox being pursued by the hounds

I got to the caravan and knocked on the door and as the gypsy opened it he looked in disbelief and shouted at the dogs to calm down. He then said, "You must be mad, you should be dead by now and how the hell did you manage to get across the yard!" I just said I had a way with dogs. I asked him about the dead horse and in typical gypsy style he denied that it was his horse.

When I got back to Harry, he was amazed I was still in one piece and said, "I tried to get in there yesterday and was too scared of the dogs and when I saw them come out of the barn at you, I thought you had had it!"

"What!" I said, "Why didn't you warn me before I went in!"

And he said, "If I'd done that, you would not have gone in."

I did not stop shaking for some hours afterwards. I drove into the field where the dead horse was lying and got an excavator to dig a deep hole to bury it. So there it remains, under one of the M25 embankments near South Ockendon.

Strange though, that if the gypsy was telling the truth about ownership, then overnight, someone must have fly-tipped a dead horse?

Chapter 36
Danger UXB

My site cabin was near the edge of a deep cutting at the M25/A13 interchange near Aveley Village and one sunny day I was doing my paperwork when Terry came to the door. He was a Bulldozer and Scraper driver removing soil from the cutting.

He said, "I've just hit a big boulder and can't shift it, can you get a concrete breaker down to break it up?"

"That's strange," I said, "There shouldn't be any boulders in this sand."

"Well I have given it a good bash and it's very heavy," Terry said, so we walked down the batter to the boulder. As I got up to it, I realised it was a UXB, a World War 2 unexploded bomb, and a big one at that.

The bomb finder

I told Terry to move his machine out of the way and stop anyone coming down into the cutting whilst I ran back to the office to phone the Army bomb disposal. We were sitting on the bank making sure that no one came into the cutting when the army boys turned up. Down the bank went one of them with a pair of stethoscopes around his neck. He bent down, put on the stethoscopes and put the other end on the bomb. He suddenly got up and ran up the slope shouting orders to his men. He stopped in front of me and said, "Clear the site, we've got a one tonne bomb with a delayed action timer and you've set it off with all your banging." – "Me?"

Is it live Doc? – Yes its ticker's going!

The police cleared the village, stopped all the traffic and we cleared the site. Apparently, it went off at around 6 o'clock that evening and shattered some windows in the village. Luckily, being in a deep cutting, most of the blast went upwards. Next day we picked up shrapnel and my mate found the clockwork timer which was as good as the day it was made, except it was a bit bent. Apparently, the timer could have been set from between 5 minutes to days or weeks and luckily for me and my men, it was set for six hours.

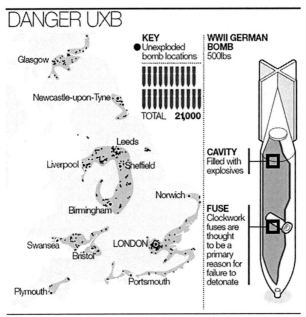

DANGER UXB

KEY
● Unexploded bomb locations

WWII GERMAN BOMB 500lbs

TOTAL **21,000**

CAVITY Filled with explosives

FUSE Clockwork fuses are thought to be a primary reason for failure to detonate

Glasgow
Newcastle-upon-Tyne
Leeds
Liverpool
Sheffield
Norwich
Birmingham
Swansea
Bristol
LONDON
Portsmouth
Plymouth

Only 20,999 more for me to find!

A week later, I was driving down the same cutting when a dumptruck went past. As I looked up at the soil in the back I noticed an anti-aircraft shell sticking up on the top. I shot around and chased it up the haul road and finally caught the driver's attention and stopped him. After clearing the area and sending someone to phone bomb disposal again, I drove back to where the soil was being excavated. The excavator driver was waiting for the dumptrucks to come back and looked puzzled as to where they had gone. "Steve," I said, "did you not see that AA shell in your bucket as you loaded the dumper?"

And he said, "Of course I saw it and thought, 'Effing hell, I need to get rid of this,' so I loaded it and sent him on his way!!!"

I thought that was a slightly selfish attitude – don't you think? Anyway, next time he found one a few days later he did the right thing and cleared the area.

The shell collector (species – Anti-Aircraft)

Chapter 37
Archaeology

During my time digging in the ground, I have carried out quite a bit of unofficial archaeology. However, my methods differ slightly from the real archaeologists because they use tiny trowels and brushes and I use massive excavators. That sentence would fill a real archaeologist with horror but if it was not for our digging machines, a lot of important sites would not have been discovered.

Do you want any help to dig out that Roman pot?

One day in 1973 I was watching our 80-tonne motor scrapers removing soil from a quarry near Chignell St James (Chelmsford) when I noticed an orange disc in the ground. I stopped the scrapers in that area and told them to scrape somewhere else whilst I investigated the strange object. After a bit of shovelling, I found six upturned bowls in a circle and under these were pots filled with burnt bones. With the bones were sandal nails and other bits of metal.

My Roman Samian Ware Bowl 75AD Central Gaul

I collected up all the broken bits and pieces and put them in a bag and took them to the Chelmsford & Essex Museum keeping back one of the bowls myself. They turned out to be Roman first-century cremations and the museum wondered why they should be buried in this remote location. A few years later, a Roman Villa was found by aerial photographs about 100 yards away on the other side of the River Can.

In 1988 whilst working at Stansted Airport my earthmovers found another Roman burial, this time it was of a high-status person as he had all the tools for the afterlife placed in a wooden box. It was thought that he was a British Chieftain who had been Romanised. This time I called in the real archaeologists and they carefully dug it all up nice and slowly and properly.

The Stansted Box Burial

Chapter 38
Land Rovers

My First experience of driving a 'Land Rover' was early March 1971. I was 20 years old at the time with my baby face and I was still being asked for proof of my age when buying a drink in a pub. The 'Land Rover' that I drove was actually a Range Rover. They had appeared on the market a few months previously and they were a rare and expensive machine. A few very rich people had them at the time.

My boss was attending a planning inquiry for a proposed new gravel quarry in north east Essex and he phoned me to say that the planning inspector wanted to visit the site the next day and because the site was quite a walk from the public highway they needed a 4X4 vehicle that could take at least four people. He said that he had arranged for me to go to a posh Land Rover dealer in West London and pick up a hired Range Rover. The idea was for me to collect it and then next morning, drive it to the town hall where the inquiry was taking place and then take the inspector to the site. It had been snowing for some days previously and the ground was very soft.

After a short underground train ride from my home in Dagenham I duly turned up at the dealer in London's West End with its big glass windows showing off a range of very expensive cars under spotlights. When I walked into the showroom the Saville Row suited manager could not believe that this diminutive baby-faced child was going to take his gleaming new Range Rover onto the streets of London. After checking with my boss that I was actually old enough to drive it he reluctantly showed me how the thing worked and handed over the keys. There seemed to be a hint of a tear in his eye. For someone who normally drove a 1960 crunch gearbox Ford Poplar, the Range Rover was fantastic. Driving through London traffic on a snowy dark evening was a bit nerve-racking but loads of fun! I arrived back home in Dagenham with rosy cheeks and a smile. My dad was very impressed.

Next morning I drove up to the Town Hall in Clacton where the inquiry was taking place and waited for the inspector. He did not come out until lunchtime with my boss and a number of others who all wanted to see the site. They were clad in wellington boots and all piled into the Range Rover and off we went to the site. As I turned into the field through a gateway, all we could see was virgin snow. I knew the track went in a straight line from the gate to the corner of a wood. The planning proposal was about creating a gravel pit within an ancient wood known as Little Bentley Hall Wood of some 130 acres. It was proposed that all the trees would be cut down in this dense woodland, leaving only a thin line of trees around the boundary. (Let me tell you at this stage, that thankfully, the plan was eventually turned down and this wonderful wood is still there!)

Off I went through the snow along the track and I soon found that it consisted of deep rutted mud. We ploughed along until we arrived at the wood, where I assumed that my passengers would all get out, but they told me to drive around inside the wood along the rides. We wallowed along, missing trees by inches with the liquid mud spraying up over the bonnet. At intervals my passengers got out and walked around squelching through the ooze. By the time we arrived back on the highway, the Range Rover was completely plastered inside and out. I took the team back to the town hall and after dropping them off made my way back to West London in the dark.

When I arrived at the posh dealer, the manager came out in his pin-striped suit to look at the vehicle. With real tears in his eyes he howled, "What the hell have you done to my Range Rover, you've wrecked it!" I explained to him that it was only mud and that after cleaning it, I was sure that there was still a good Range Rover underneath.

As I got onto the underground train with all the hundreds of commuters, I noticed they were all looking at me in a strange way. I looked down and saw that I still had my wellington boots on and was also plastered in mud, which is not something you often see in central London!

Looking back on the incident now I can understand the manager's dismay at the state of his expensive Range Rover but it just goes to show that a complete prat can drive one in the worst of conditions and still get away with it!

In 1978 I badgered my company for a Land Rover as I kept getting stuck in the mud on site. They told me that I would not like a proper van-type Land Rover because they were noisy and uncomfortable. Still I badgered until one day after a bit of under the counter dealings (they were difficult to get hold of) my new blue and cream Land Rover turned up. I would never admit it to my boss but it was a shock when I drove it for the first time. It was so noisy you could not hear yourself think and if it went over a matchstick, you certainly felt it! Anyway I came to love the thing and I have had Land Rovers in many guises ever since. They have saved my bacon lots of times and I will relate a few of my adventures here.

I did 120,000 miles in my first Landy and used it to its full four-wheel drive potential. The M25 started in 1979 and I was the project manager on three contracts which spanned over 10 miles. Walking the site was not an option so I usually drove up and down the site most of the day, managing the earthworks. In wet weather the site was a quagmire but it was rare for me to get stuck. However, when I did get stuck it was usually for a good reason, such as being perched on top of a tree stump, stuck down the bottom of a deep ditch or buried in a quicksand. A good tug from a bulldozer always got me out of trouble.

One morning it was icy and I was driving to the site around the back lanes near Brentwood when I thought, *I should slow down, it's a bit too icy*. Not heeding my own thoughts I went down a hill in a narrow lane when suddenly a Ford Sierra came the other way. We both braked and slid sideways and crashed side by side. The Sierra almost exploded as the windscreen and side windows shattered. As the noise died down I slid my side window open and the guy looked up at me through a windowless hole and told me he was OK. We wriggled ourselves away from each other and both got out. His car was wrecked but mine only had a small scratch on the cill under the door. We both admitted that it was knock for knock and he was not concerned as he worked for Ford and it was a company car. I towed him up the road into a layby and took him to his office in Warley. I pulled the cill back into position and drove off to work. Land Rovers are strong vehicles!

Chapter 39
Don't Worry Beth

I was driving back to our stables from a long distance horse ride with my sister-in-law Beth when we turned down the narrow lane to the stables. A car came in the opposite direction and I pulled over onto the verge. As the car drove past the Land Rover slid in slow motion sideways into the deep ditch. I looked down at Beth and said, "Don't worry, Beth, I'll put it in four-wheel drive and we'll get out OK." As I did so, all four wheels went around in mid-air – we were stuck. I opened my door, got up onto the cill and pulled Beth up and out.

Green grass against the passenger window blue sky in the other

We walked into the stable yard and I asked Paul, the son of the owner, if he could bring his Land Rover to pull us out. Everyone in the yard came to watch and sat on the banks around the operation. Paul attached some large chains to my Landy and slowly pulled – all that happened was his wheels spun round.

After a few goes, he said that there was nothing for it but to reverse back to mine and go flat out.

I thought that he would either pull the back off mine, his one or both. He reversed and accelerated hard. There was an almighty bang as the chains became taught and my Landy popped out of the ditch. Huge clapping and cheering came from the gathered crowd.

Chapter 40
The Swimming Landy

I have had many adventures when driving a Land Rover and it is not often I have got myself stuck. I have often driven through fords and deep water and the key here is to keep the throttle going so that the water cannot be sucked up the exhaust pipe into the engine. Even when changing gear, the throttle needs to be kept high.

After some very heavy rain, I was driving to work through the lanes near the village of Matching when I came across a winding flooded lane. It had deep ditches on both sides which were full of water and the road was covered in about a foot of water. I waded the Landy through with no trouble. It had stopped raining during the day and I came home the same way but by this time it was very dark.

As I came up to the flooded lane, I had no conception that the water may have risen, so I went forward slowly into the water. All was going well, until I went round a bend and the water got suddenly deeper and deeper. There was no going back as I could not reverse along the winding lane in the dark and anyway, by now my reversing light was below water level. I kept going forward and just as I came to the next bend, the water came over the bonnet and the lights went out! It was pitch black, in a winding lane with deep ditches on each side and there was no going back. If I stopped, the engine would draw in the floodwater and I would be stranded. My only hope then would be for me to try and wade back up to my waist, to dry land, in the dark. My chance of survival was slim in the freezing water, so I kept going trying to make out the hedges on both sides and to stay in the middle of the road. I was revving the engine and slipping the clutch and sweating. Eventually, the water became shallower and as I reached dry land, the lights slowly came back on. Phew!

A real brown underpants moment

Chapter 41
The Dyke

Essex has many islands off its east coast and they are all flat with few trees and buildings. They are criss-crossed by wide deep dykes and I was managing the construction of a new sea defence wall on one of the larger ones by using the soft alluvial soil which caused us all sorts of difficulties. When it rained, the soft soil became instantly slippery like ice and even walking on it was fraught with an A over T moment.

One day I wanted to look at the next section of works which was further across the island, so together with my foreman George, I drove my Discovery along a flat berm between the sea wall and a dyke at a walking pace. All was going fine until we suddenly had a shower of rain and as I went round a bend in the track, the Disco slid ever so slowly towards the dyke. It finally stopped on the edge with one wheel on my side just on the edge of the dyke. I looked down in horror at the water six foot below and probably six foot deep.

George panicked and said, "I'm out of here!" and went to open his door at which point I grabbed him and said,

"Your weight is the only thing stopping this car going over the edge with me in it, so stay where you are!" He agreed and stayed put but suggested that we were both 'Doooomed!' Shades of Dad's Army.

A twin brown underpants moment!

I put the Disco in reverse and as I tried to go back all that happened was that it slid further over the edge. George was getting very worried but I kept trying to wriggle the wheels onto a non-slippery bit to get some hold. Slowly, slowly, I managed to ease the Disco back from the edge a few inches and then it would suddenly slide back to the edge. By this time George was in a bit of a sweat and confirming that we were definitely 'Doooomed!' I was turning the steering wheel slowly and at the same time reversing very carefully, then suddenly the wheels caught a bit of dry soil and eventually it gradually came away from the edge of the dyke and back onto the track. George had gone silent and I looked over to him and said, "That was a close one!" I managed to turn the car around and I very slowly drove back to the dry land keeping well away from the edge of the dyke. George told me that he had never been so scared in all his life and he never got into a car with me again. Dunno why.

Chapter 42
The Estate Car

A year after I became self-employed in 2002, my Discovery started to break down regularly and I decided to change it for another vehicle. New Land Rovers were too expensive for me, so I decided to buy a Subaru estate car. As soon as I got it, I felt that I was sitting too low compared to a Land Rover and was not overly happy with it. However, I had bought it and had to persevere with it.

One day I had a skip delivered to my home and had it plonked onto the area where I usually reversed my car. Each day I had to be careful about how I reversed to avoid the skip. It had to happen, didn't it? – One morning I came out of the house to go to a meeting in Peterborough and said goodbye to Gill and got into the car, started the engine, put it into reverse and was thinking which way I should go when – CRASH! An almighty explosion occurred as the back window caved inwards! I got out and looked at the stove in back of the Subaru. Walking back down the path to the house with my briefcase in hand, Gill said, "What's up, not going to Peterborough?"

"Na!" I said, "Decided not to go." I sold the estate car as soon as I had got it repaired and got another Land Rover...

I remembered the Cortina estate car's back door(s)!

Chapter 43
Helping the Hedge Trimmer

I have always had an inclination to help someone who needs it and one day in 1976 I was driving my yellow Cortina back to the office when I rounded a bend on the A414 near Leaden Roding. A man was standing on the verge thumbing a lift, so I stopped and asked him where he wanted to go. He told me that he had to get to Leaden Roding Hall a few miles up the road. So off we set and I asked what he had been doing and he said that he had been trimming hedges with a billhook. At this point my often 'delayed action' mind noticed that he was holding his arm and was looking a bit in pain. I looked down and saw the rubber floor mat full of blood. "Jesus!" I said, "What have you done?" He explained that he had been slashing the hedges and missed and the billhook cut his arm badly. "I can see that," I said. "You should go to hospital, I'll take you there."

"No! I must go to the Hall, they will sort me out." I put my foot down and sped along the road.

When I got to the Hall and pulled into the driveway we saw a man who took the poor lad away to be repaired. They had a pond and I thought I would clean the rubber floor mat in it. As it was frozen, I had to break the ice and then I carefully carried the mat to the pond trying not to get blood all over me. The carpets under the mat were soaked and it took ages for me to clean it and I don't think I ever did.

Chapter 44
Helping the Snowman

The winter of 1982 was very snowy and as I knew the M25 works would be shut down, I decided to make my way to my head office in Harlow. The good thing about having a Land Rover is that you can drive in deep snow; however, the bad thing is that all the people with two wheel drive vehicles also try to drive to work and get completely stuck. I knew that all the main roads would have long queues of cars all stuck and going nowhere, so I decided to drive around the back lanes.

It took me about four hours to do a 45-minute journey to get to the office because I spent most of my time pulling cars out of ditches and snow drifts. Some of the drifts were as high as the Landy but I could bulldoze my way through. One young lad in a mini thought I was going too slowly near Stansted Airport so he overtook me at speed only to go through a hedge into a garden and he crashed into a shed. Wickedly, I stopped as he got out and hooted and waved as I drove off. Score 1–0. When I arrived at my office my managing director (who lived next door to the office) told me that he was not very happy that I had taken so long to get to work! Score 1–1.

When I left work, it was dark and snowing, so I retraced my route around the back lanes as I knew the main roads would again be jammed solid. The journey was not too bad as all the two-wheel-drive cars had decided to go home early or abandoned them on the side of the road. I drove along the open roads behind Andrewsfield airfield thinking that I must go to the stables in Shalford to do the horses when something caught my eye out of the side window. I stopped and through the blizzard I could just make out a shape moving across a field. I had to blink as the snow swept into my eyes, but there was someone walking or stumbling across the field coming towards me.

Eventually, the man got to the Landy and I told him to get in. He was covered in snow and frozen. He told me that he had left his MG sports car on the A120 and decided to walk across the fields to get home. He was about to lie down and give up when he saw my Landy through the blizzard and hoped that I would wait for him. He lived halfway between Shalford and Wethersfield, so we set off bashing my way through the snowdrifts. I got him to within 50 yards of his house where we met a real humdinger of a drift. It was 10 foot high and I tried to ram it but got stuck. We both got out and he offered to help me but I declined as I thought he should get into a warm home with his family, so I helped him over the drift to his gate and left him.

Is that a human being?

When I got back, the Landy had almost disappeared under snow, so I got the shovel out and after half an hour I managed to get it extracted and turn around. I made my way to the stables and found that Sherry, the stables owner had broken her wrist by slipping over and was in plaster. The two of us had to muck out, rug up and feed all the 20 horses including breaking the ice off their water buckets. I cannot remember when I got home but it was quite a hard day.

Chapter 45
The Next Day in the Snow

I offered to come back to the stables the next day to help Sherry as the snow was coming down quicker and thicker (that's a long way to say blizzard). We made sure all the horses were mucked out, warm and well fed and went in for a cup of tea, just as the phone rang. It was Sherry's friend Georgina who lived in Blackmore End asking if Sherry knew anyone who could get some provisions for her and the rest of the hamlet and then take them there as they were all snowed in. Sherry looked at me and said, "I've got Mike here with his Land Rover, we'll do it; what do you want?"

I set off to the Wethersfield stores with Sherry and eventually we arrived through the drifts. The blizzard was getting worse and the drifts were getting higher even though some snowploughs had gone through. We loaded up the Landy with food and other items and set off towards Blackmore End up the Hedingham Road. When we got up into the open section of road we hit a drift which stopped us dead. I got out into the blizzard with a shovel and started to dig away the snow from behind me as it was obvious that we were not going to go forward. Sherry got out and was no help with her broken wrist but she was covered in snow within seconds so I told her to get back inside. Every shovelful I dug was immediately replaced with more snow. After 20 minutes, I was exhausted and got back into the Landy. "We're well and truly stuck, Sherry!"

I contemplated what we should do but after thinking how much trouble the poor chap got into the day before, walking was not an option especially with Sherry's wrist. Just then, Sherry said, "What's that coming towards us?" I looked through the blizzard and saw a large black shape and as it slowly came closer we realised it was a lorry. When it arrived, it turned out to be a 4x4 TK Bedford ex-army truck owned by the potato factory in

Blackmore End. They stopped and said, "Want a push?" We explained that we needed to get provisions to Blackmore End and they told us that that was what they were doing and they had a list to get from the village stores, so we gave them all our goods and they all pushed me clear of the drift.

I was in reverse gear and decided not to stop until we reached the village, so I was driving backwards with my head out of the side window looking where I was going. Suddenly, a man and his wife came into view in the middle of the road and I shouted, "Get out of the way I'm not stopping!" As I got close the lady jumped to the left and the man jumped to his right... and he completely disappeared down a deep ditch. As I went past I shouted sorry to the head sticking out of the snow. I hoped that the potato people got him out...

Can't stop or I'll get stuck again

Chapter 46
Laying Down on the Railway Line

As you are by now aware, I have done some silly things in my life and this story is defiantly one that you must never recreate. Do not mess about on railway lines as they have a nasty habit of squashing you. Placing halfpennies on the line was fun but we were very careful that a train was not going to hit us. There are now videos on YouTube of boys playing chicken with trains and people trying to beat a train at a level crossing. This shows me that the modern generation has no respect for real danger. Charles Darwin's theory of 'The survival of the fittest' should also include 'The survival of the most intelligent' or 'The survival of the ones with common sense'. The alternative is to get yourself a Guardian Angel like me, but I imagine they are hard to come by.

One snowy Saturday we decided to visit a friend who lived near the branch railway line which runs from Marks Tey near Colchester to Sudbury in Suffolk. Our little group consisted of my wife Gill, her sister Beth and her future husband Tony. We arrived at our friend's farmhouse in my Land Rover having battled our way through the snowdrifts and our friend, Sheila asked if we wanted to go to the local pub for lunch. We started to walk to the pub but were thwarted by some high snowdrifts. "Let's walk along the railway line," said Sheila, "The trains won't be running today, they stop them even if they have a leaf on the line." So off we went onto the railway line and picked our way along the slippery sleepers.

After a few snowball fights, we decided that Beth should lay down on the tracks and we could pretend to tie her up and then Tony could come to her rescue.

We were giggling at Beth protesting about laying on the tracks when suddenly we heard a loud blaring sound and looked around and saw a train coming straight towards us. "Oh buddy hell!" We all carefully but quickly stepped off the rail lines just in time to see the driver mouthing something to us and making rude gestures. In unison we mouthed, "SORRY."

"Ooh, that's strange," said Sheila, "I didn't think they would be running trains today."

"When is the next one?" I asked.

"Not for another hour," she said.

"Oh, that's good we can keep going but we have to work out the times of the trains when we come back… and be a bit more careful when trying to tie Beth to the railway lines."

Chapter 47
Stranded

The winter of 2000/2001 was particularly wet and I was going to see my brother who had cancer and lived in Hertfordshire. Firstly I had to travel down to Upminster to pick up my mother and sister, so I went the country way through Cressing towards White Notley. As I came down the hill into Notley the river was in full flood but it had a little bridge over it so you didn't need to use the ford. I noticed that in the middle of the ford, a young couple was standing on the roof of a car trying to climb up onto the bridge.

A prat on a cold tin roof

I stopped and helped them climb up onto the bridge. They were soaked to the skin and frozen so I gave the young lady a coat to put on. I asked the guy how he managed to get into the ford and he said that he had just picked up his new BMW company car and was taking his girlfriend for a ride when they came to the ford, so he thought he would try to go through rather than over the bridge. What a prat!

He asked me if I could tow him out before the water swept in under the bridge and I told him that he would have to fix the tow rope to the car as I did not want to damage his car further and it was his responsibility. I suggested that he must have a towing ring in the boot so he waded into the water to find it. He opened the boot and rummaged around for some time in the murky water before locating it. His hands and arms were cut badly from rummaging around in the strong current and I waded into the river up to my wellies to help him out.

By this time the police had turned up, but they were only useful in controlling the minimal amount of traffic as they were not willing to help with the recovery and they did not even have a first-aid kit. I bandaged the poor chaps' arms and hands just as the river moved his car towards the bridge. It would not be long before it went under and lost forever. I told him that it was now or never and he had to go back into the water and screw the towing ring into the bumper of the car and attach the tow rope. He was very brave and after some while he did it and I hooked the rope onto the Landy. The car was full of water and as we opened the doors, a torrent came out. I bandaged up his soaked arms and hands again and left him waiting for the ambulance the police had called. I wonder what his boss said to him about the wrecked Beamer.

As I continued my journey to see my brother, rather late, I was thinking what an idiot he had been when I realised that someone else I knew not very far away had gone through a flooded lane in the dark…

Chapter 48
Road Rage – The Scotsman

I seem to attract the attention of angry drivers and I think some people get up in the morning being angry and stay angry all day. Road rage seems to have increased as the number of vehicles have increased and during my earlier driving days I was not too much aware of this strange phenomenon (unless I tried to run them over and then I could understand it!)

An early incident sticks out when I was driving along the A13 in East London in my yellow Cortina when I must have done something to upset a Scottish man driving an articulated lorry, because he suddenly overtook me against all the oncoming traffic and stopped in front of me. He got out and I wound the window down to see what the problem was and he stuck his head through it only an inch away from my face and was shouting in Scottish at me. He was screaming all these untruths at me, telling me that I was a Cockney (not true as I was not born within the sound of Bow bells), that my mother was obviously not married (yes she is, she has a certificate to prove it), that I was ugly (may be true), that I did not know how to drive (yes I did as I had a licence) and other naughty things.

Becoming a bit bored listening to his rantings, I decided to wind up the window and drive off – with his head still in my face, so I reached down and started winding. He was in such a rage he did not realise what was happening until the glass contacted his neck. At this point I started to move off and his face went from red to purple. He started to beat the door panel with his fists at which point I decided that if I wanted to keep a door on the car, I should wind down the window. I left him in the middle of the road clutching his neck and still shouting that my mother was not married. The door had to be panel beaten to iron out all the dents.

Chapter 49
Road Rage – Druggies

Besides the usual hooting, mouthing and gesticulating that seems to be the norm nowadays, two other incidents stick out as being particularly frightening. My makeup tells me that I should stand up to bullies without trying to overdo it and get myself into trouble. However, drug crazed people cannot to be reasoned with and their false strength can be far too much for a little person like me to handle.

Driving up to a mini roundabout towards home one evening, I looked right and saw a car coming towards me about 100 yards away. As he was not near the roundabout, I pulled out and turned left. As I pulled away along the road, he came up behind me and hooted and I looked in my rear view mirror and saw this mad man, red in the face and giving victory signs.

As I came up to a pedestrian crossing, a young lady with a pram was about to cross, so I stopped and he overtook me and missed the pram by a hairs breath. The lady and I looked at each other and we both pulled an astonished face. As I moved off I realised that he had stopped to wait for me in the road and as I drove towards him, he moved off slowly. I followed him along the road and he suddenly stopped which caused me to brake hard. He had his arm out of the window making further victory signs and shouting and he was not going to move. He had now made me annoyed by nearly running over the baby in a pram and now this, so I carefully drove forward and buttoned up my bumper to his. I then put the Landy in low gear box and drove forward pushing him along the road with his brakes locked on and the tyres scrubbing along the tarmac. This now made him even madder and he suddenly drove off and 100 yards later stopped again. As I drove up he got out of the car and I immediately realised that he was high on drugs. I locked the doors as he came up to the window and started bashing it with his fists. I could see the glass bending inwards and he was going totally berserk and screaming.

I was trying to keep calm as I phoned the police and within 5 minutes two police cars had arrived and he then turned on them. It took three of them to get him on the ground and hold him down. The other policeman asked me what had happened and he said that the man was known to them and the best thing would be for me to drive off and leave it to them to sort out.

While all this was going on I had also phoned my wife Gill and she had walked down the road to see what all the fuss was about. She joined the onlookers as the scene was played out and watched while the woman passenger in the mad man's car got out and walked off leaving matey to the police. A large whisky was in order when I got home.

A similar occurrence came a few years ago when I took Gill into Braintree town and as I came up to a line of parked cars, I stopped to wait for a lorry coming in the opposite direction. Suddenly there was lots of tooting behind me and as the lorry drove past, a car overtook me by going up onto the pavement and roared off up the road. He then stopped in the middle of the road, got out and waited for me to catch up. He then walked up to my window shouting and screaming that I should not have stopped to let the lorry through and this apparently, was a stupid act on my part. His face was bright red and his bulging eyes were blood shot. I turned to Gill and said he must be on drugs.

He then drove off along the dead end road into a car park and was waiting for me again with his girlfriend, still in a rage. He accosted me again through the locked windows, bashing them with his fists. He then jumped on the bonnet as I moved off and the thought did cross my mind to run him over, but I restrained myself. Eventually he walked off and the police came after I had phoned them. As I described him to them with his star tattoos on his neck, they told me he was known to them and they would put out a call to apprehend him in the town.

Gill, there's a druggie on the bonnet!

We decided that shopping in Braintree that day could wait so we drove to Sudbury instead with Gill telling me that Braintree was full of dreadful people and Sudbury had all nice types of people in it. As we walked into Waitrose, there was a scuffle and two security men had a man on the floor with bottles of stolen Whisky in his pockets.

I felt like going over to them and asking if I could have a large one please…

Chapter 50
The Angry Gypsies

In 1997 I was asked to carry out a job clearing a mound of soil from an established gypsy site in Thurrock. The mound was in the far corner of the site and the internal roads were very narrow and went around in a playing card shape with caravans all the way round. The Traveller Liaison Officer for Thurrock Council explained that the gypsies would not be happy with the intrusion of diggers and lorries coming into 'their' place and we would have to be particularly careful when we did the work.

On the day of the job I got all the lorry drivers together with the digger driver and told them to drive very slowly around the roads, give way to everyone and just be very careful not to upset any of the residents. I watched the first lorries going at less than walking pace along the roads with the digger carefully placing the soil into the lorries rather than dumping it and making any noise or dust. I decided that it was going OK and saw the big boss gypsy man with the standard braces and belt etc., just to make sure he was happy. He was, so I drove away down the road.

Five minutes – yes, five minutes down the road I got a phone call from the digger driver in a panic telling me I had better come back as all hell had broken loose and they were going to be killed by the gypsies! "Calm down!" I said, "Tell me what has happened."

And he said, "One of the lorries got too close to a kerb and the tyre had blown with a bang. It was next to a low brick wall and the air pressure had blown some bricks across the front garden then they smashed through a caravan window over a cot where a baby was sleeping and then across the room and had smashed a mirror!"

BANG! Crunch! Wheee! Crash! Smash!

It could not have been worse if you really tried to cause a riot. Driving back, I summoned up all my diplomatic skills and more. Turning into the site, the gypsy boss was waiting with a crowd of other gypsies. All my brave drivers were locked safely in their cabs leaving me to sort out the problem. The baby was shoved in my face with brick dust on it, the mother was screaming so much I could not make out what she was saying, their menfolk were explaining that I would have to die very slowly at their hands and all the women were joining in as well while my men looked on from the safety of their cabs.

Luckily, the big boss man came to my rescue with offers of money – not from him but from me to them. I was dragged into the caravan to assess how much the repairs would cost to put right plus the stress and worry from the mother, plus the stress and worry from all the other residents and of course the near-death experience of the baby and all the seven years bad luck that will befall the family now they have a smashed mirror in their caravan.

We finished the work and all the income from it went straight to the boss man to share out to his people. My drivers thought I did a very good job of not getting them killed though!

Chapter 51
'What Am I Doing Here'
Situation – Iraqis

Have you been in one of those situations when you've said to yourself, 'What the hell am I doing here?' That thought has occurred to me on many occasions.

In the early 1990s my managing director had a meeting in London with an Arab gentleman. He was a middleman for the Baghdad Contracting Company (I'm not making it up – honest). They could not buy American earthmoving machines because there was an embargo on exporting to Iraq and in those days China had not started making them for export. The USA was the only country you could get 80 tonne motor scrapers and large D9 bulldozers. This gent was looking for a British company to purchase and sell them a fleet of second hand scrapers and dozers. The middleman's fee was 10% of the total deal cost, a nice flat in Mayfair during the transaction, a new Mini car and sufficient 'Ladies' to satisfy his needs – Oh, and a well-stocked drinks cabinet.

My MD came back cock-a-hoop and started to locate all the large equipment he could get his hands on. Once purchased it all came to our workshops to be refurbished and painted yellow with 'Baghdad Contracting Co.' on them. There was just one other proviso in the deal, just a small one…None of the equipment, spares or any other items must have been supplied, handled, made or delivered by a Jew or Jewish company. He was told that if he wanted an export/import licence into Iraq, that it was their condition as the infidels were their sworn enemy. "No problem," said our MD.

A motorscraper – 80 tonnes of thundering steel – doing 40 mph. No cab – no seat belt – no brakes – no health & safety – GREAT!

The day came when the first two machines were ready to be exported and the MD came into my office. "Mike, can you go to the Iraqi embassy and get this export/import licence signed?"

"Of course!" I said.

"Oh, one other thing, you also have to take this affidavit with you stating that Jews have not been involved with anything to do with these machines, then you have to sign it in front of them, we have made you our official representative."

"Oh, ta," I said and followed with, "Has any Jew been involved?"

And he said, "Of course they have, we would never have been able to get these sorted out without the help of Jews or Jewish made parts, but the Iraqis don't know that, so it's alright." Hum!

So up to London I went and found the Iraqi embassy in Queens Gate. The young girl on the reception desk was a very attractive Arab and it was a pleasure to get her to counter sign my signature on the affidavit and hand me the stamped export/import licence. I had to go back on a number of occasions, looking forward to seeing Miss Arabic 1990 again.

Then the day came for the last licence to be stamped. I turned up at reception and the attractive Arab girl said, "Hallo Mr Sarling. How are you today?" *All the better for seeing you*, I thought and handed her the documents as usual. "Ah," she said,

"Mr (Arab sounding name), wants to do these last ones, follow me." So I did, down along the corridors, down the steps into the basement and along another corridor. At this point I thought that if this guy was legitimate, he would have an office in the main upstairs building not down this ever increasingly dark corridor. Then the thought occurred to me, *Have they found out that I have been lying about the non-Jewish affidavit?* Oh, sesame seed, this girl is taking me to my doom. I may never be seen again, having been smuggled out in a diplomatic bag – in bits!

Into the Iraqi dungeons

Eventually I was shown into this dimly lit room with just a desk and a chair, the girl left and closed the door and Mr Arab sounding name told me to sit down. I looked around the room to see if his henchmen were hiding in the shadows when he said, "Mr Sarling, I am so pleased to meet you, you have helped my country a lot and I just wanted to say thank you in person." And he held out his hand for me to shake it. After we signed the documents and he stamped the stamps, he told me to find my own way out, thanking me again. Had I been filmed signing the affidavit? Will they get me before I reached the exit?

I emerged into the London sunshine and stood on the pavement telling myself that I would not do that again for all the tea in China.

Chapter 52
'What Am I Doing Here'
Situation – Vegetables

I was working on the London Olympics Athletes Village project in East London and was driving to the site, waiting at a set of traffic lights, when this black Range Rover started hooting the traffic around him. As the lights went to green, he cut up a number of cars and then clipped mine in the back. I got out and he wound the window down and this dusky looking gent said, "Sorry, I'm in a rush, all my fault, here is my card, bring me the bill, I shall pay you in cash," and with that he drove off.

I looked at the card and it was from a Mr Cypriot sounding name, Stand 00 New Spittlefields Market Wholesale Fruit and Veg dealer. *Well, this is alright,* I thought, I shall just get a written quotation and get the money off him – no probs.

I got a quotation for £600 and drove into the market car park one morning about 9 o'clock. The car park was nearly empty except for masses of fruit and vegetables scattered all over it. It was obvious that the market starts early in the morning and finishes early. I parked the car and went into the vast market shed looking for stand 00.

I was getting some funny looks from the remaining guys walking about but I eventually found stand 00. There was a bunch of dusky looking guys at the entrance and I walked up to them and said, "I am looking for Mr Popalupudos (or something)."

"Ooo vonts to no?" said one.

"Ah, he drove into my car and I have come to pick up some money," I said.

"Vaate dere," the biggest one said and he went into the back. Out he came and said, "Follow me." We went down a corridor into a dark and dingy back office where a group of rough looking men were crammed in and behind a big desk was the man who bashed my car.

"Hallo Mr Popa whats it, I've got a quotation for my car and you said you would pay for it in cash."

He retorted, "I thought you would have forgotten about it, are you sure it was me and was it my fault, I seem to remember it was yours." I looked around and the men all had a funny smirk on their faces.

He then turned a bit aggressive when I said, "No, it was you who hit my car and the quotation is for £600."

The man started to turn nasty and said, "What, you must be joking, £50 more like it, you must know a repair man to get a dodgy quote like that!"

I was getting a bit nervous of the situation but I said, "I can assure you I don't and you told me to get a quotation so here it is."

He stood up and said, "I'm not paying you that in cash, you'll have to go through my insurers."

Surrounded by fruit and veg men

"Can I have your insurance details then?" I said and he rummaged around in his desk and wrote something on a piece of paper, handed it to me and told me to go. As I turned around and walked out I could feel the men around me getting a bit fractious. I walked in a straight line, out of the shed and back to my car.

What did I find written on the paper – just some letters and a number, nothing else. I was not beat though but I was not going back to the guy. The number started with a 'Z' and I thought perhaps this could be the first letter of the insurance company such as Zurich. I phoned them and explained my predicament and they told me that it was theirs and they would send me the forms to fill in.

It was all sorted out professionally by them and I got paid out OK. However, it was the first and last time I was scared of a vegetable man.

Chapter 53
'What Am I Doing Here'
Situation – Vandals

Apparently, my wife Gill told off some young lads not to ride their bicycles down the footpath next to our house. She had had some complaints that footpath users and their dogs had nearly been run over.

Some years later, whilst watching telly one evening we heard a crashing sound coming from the footpath and I saw three boys breaking our wooden fence down. I rushed out to confront them but they scarpered down the footpath towards the farm.

Looking at the flattened fence, I decided to get in my car and drive around to the other end of the footpath about half a mile away to cut off their escape. Off I went and when I got to the end there was no sign of them, so I started to drive up the path back towards home. Suddenly my headlights picked out three youths walking towards me. I stopped the car and got out and waited for them.

As they got closer, I said, "Now then you boys, what did you smash down my fence for?" At this point, I realised that the three 'boys' were about six foot tall.

"Cos your wife told us off some years back for riding our bikes down here we came down to get our own back," said the biggest one. *Keep cool and upright, Mike*, I thought, here I am in the middle of a field in the pitch black confronting three angry teenagers at least a foot taller than me.

What to do? I thought. "Right, give me your names and addresses," I said.

"Wot dew fink we are, stoopid or someink?" said the big one. So I gave them a lecture on the rights and wrongs of what they had done and told them that it will cost me a lot of money to put the damage right and what were they going to do about it.

I tried to lecture my way out of the situation

At any point they could have bashed me and left me there, but they didn't, I was lucky. They then walked off down the path saying things like, 'Soppy old man if he thought he could take us on' etc.

The fence was on its last legs anyway so I had a new one erected but we did not have any more trouble from the ~~little~~ large vandals.

Chapter 54
Burglars

Our home has been burgled on three occasions (to date). The first time, they turned up when we were out for the evening and stripped the house of all the valuables including furniture, Gill's jewellery and all the bits and pieces that we had inherited and collected and can never be replaced. They did a good job that evening.

Then our garage and car was broken into but the car alarm went off when they smashed the windows and this woke us up and they scarpered leaving a trail of stolen goods across our field behind the house.

Next, Gill came back from a walk on a hot day and decided to change into shorts so she went upstairs into the bedroom and found a man behind the door. "What the hell do you think you are doing?" she said and he replied that he was burgling her house! She made him turn out his pockets and then when he got to the bottom of the stairs she told him to wait for her to phone the police. He begged her not to as he was on bail but that did not stop her. The place was surrounded by policemen within a few minutes and they arrested him, on this and other charges. It turned out that he was a member of the notorious Kray gang in the 1960s and had spent most of his life in prison. Gill didn't get a medal but she should have.

And then there was the mystery one…

One foggy night we had the bedroom window open and about two in the morning I woke up and heard a creaking sound as if someone was using a crowbar to break into a door. Creak-creak-creak it went and then it would stop and then start again. I stood at the window trying to make out where it was coming from through the fog. In the end I was convinced it was coming from Bob's garden who lived a few doors down from us.

I threw on some clothes and phoned Bob. A sleepy Bob answered the phone and said, "Ooo is it!"

"It's Mike and someone is trying to break into your shed with a crowbar, go and have a look." A few minutes later he came back and said that he could not see because of the fog but could hear the noise. I told him that if I went through our field and around to his back garden and he came out of his back door, then if the burglar tried to escape I could stop him. He agreed and I told him to give me a few minutes to get into position.

Common sense then took over and I thought, *What if this bloke was 10 foot tall and was armed with a crowbar?* So I got my air rifle for protection and went outside, ever so quietly. I crept down my path to my field and went to climb over the post and rail fence. I got one foot over, when suddenly both feet slipped on the wet timber rail and my crotch came down and hit the top rail, and at the same time the rifle came up and smacked me in the side of my head. Usually, I would utter some choice words but I had to keep quiet so as not to alert the burglar.

Crunch – smack! My crotch went down as the gun came up

Walking along the backs of the gardens holding my sore crotch and face plus the rifle, I got to the rear fence of Bob's garden, where he was waiting. "There is no one here Mike, are you sure that it was a burglar?" I very carefully climbed over his fence into the garden and stood next to his rabbit hutch, just as the large rabbit inside started to chew the wood – creak, creak, creak it went.

Chapter 55
Guns – The Rat

Guns – they are very dangerous implements, especially in my hands. Some years ago we kept chickens in a very large chicken house known as 'The Pavilion.' It looked like the cricket pavilion at Lords Cricket ground. It was made from corrugated iron sheets with Georgian windows painted green and white and was bolted to a concrete floor. In the 1987 hurricane it took off and landed in the farmers' field behind our stables looking just like the tangled wreckage of an aeroplane crash. Some of the chickens were still hanging on for dear life on their perches, not in the crashed pavilion but the ones still fixed to the concrete floor where it had been.

Anyway, I am going off the point of this story. One day I went into the pavilion and a rat ran along the back wall down a beam and into a hole in the concrete. The little brown jobbie had been playing merry hell with our chicks, so it had to go. I tried a rattrap (like a spring mousetrap but larger) and caught a blackbird which made me more annoyed about the rat. I could not put down poison as the chickens would eat it so I filled in the hole with concrete.

Next day I went down and the rat ran along the back wall down a beam and into a hole in the concrete. The little brown jobbie had eaten away the wet concrete! This was now war and I came up with a cunning plan. The rat was a rodent of habit and it took the same route along the back wall, down a beam and into a hole in the concrete as soon as I opened the door. The time between it starting its run and entering the hole was about two seconds, so all I had to do was to open the door, point my air rifle at the hole, wait for it to get there and fire – easy.

The day came to dispatch the little brown job. I crept down to the pavilion, opened the door and matey started its run, I aimed at the hole and just as it got there I fired. Bang! whizz, smack into the hole, missed the thing and the pellet ricocheted out of the hole and hit me in the knee! I dropped the rifle, swore, told the rat that it was an ugly little banana and went back to the house to get the hole in my knee patched up.

It could have ricocheted anywhere – but no – it had to be my knee

147

Chapter 56
Guns – The Pheasant

Shotguns are even better for having accidents with. I have done all the usual damage to myself like splitting my thumb on the barrel opening catch because I fired when my thumb was in the way. Cor! That was a lot of blood and we were in the middle of a pheasant drive so I had to keep shooting with blood squirting everywhere. Then climbing over a barbed wire fence and – no not shooting myself, because I always unload the gun when I am not actually shooting! – No this was me being halfway over the fence when I slipped and grabbed the fence leaving holes in my gloves and my hands. These sort of accidents are common in the shooting field…aren't they?

Don't worry – no birds were harmed in this photo
I'm a rotten shot!

One day I was invited to a shoot near Brightlingsea. At the start of the day, the Guns (the ones who are shooting that day) pick a hidden number from a set of sticks or cards. Before the shoot, the gamekeeper will have pushed stakes into the ground (called pegs) around each drive. Each peg has a number on it and each Gun goes to his or her number and shoots from that position. On the next drive each Gun goes up two numbers and goes to that peg. In this way each Gun has an even chance of getting a good or a poor place where the birds will fly out from.

Once each Gun is on the peg, the Beaters (the ones who are not shooting) flush the birds out of the woods or cover hopefully towards the Guns by shouting, beating the trees with sticks or flapping a plastic flag. However, the birds usually fly in all directions.

Towards the end of the day my peg was situated well away from the other guns in a remote spot the other side of a wood. I was standing in the middle of a field hearing the other guns shooting but with no pheasants coming my way when suddenly I heard one squawking and it was approaching me over the tops of the high trees. Then I saw it through the tree tops about 100 foot up and I laid my gun on it. As it emerged into the open…Bang! I fired and immediately saw that it was dead in the air. A nice, clean shot.

I instinctively looked down and broke my gun to add another cartridge into the barrel when I looked up and saw, at the last second, the dead pheasant hurdling towards my face. I just had time to turn my head as the four-pound pheasant smacked me in my right ear. It knocked me sideways and to the ground and as I went to get up a soggy muddy Labrador crashed into me and picked up the bird and ran back from whence it came.

The pheasant got its own back on me

Night seemed to come quickly as I actually saw stars. Of course when the whistle blew for the drive to be over and I returned to the other guns, they thought I was joking until I showed them the claw marks and blood in my ear. Concussion ensued for a day or so.

Chapter 57
Guns – The Maternity Hospital

I used to compete in a team event called a Field Sports Triathlon. This was not like the Olympics where fit and healthy people swim, run and jump – no, this was for unfit people like me who would form a team of three so that we could jump horses over fences, cast fishing fly's and shoot clay pigeons. As an aside after trying to improve over many years our team actually won the national championships. Apologies for bragging but after that they cancelled the event!

Anyway, we used to do intensive training for each element and my friends Gerry & Connie had a clay trap layout on their land and allowed us to use them to practice our clay shooting. One evening, one of our team members was late so Kate, my other team mate and I went out to the shooting ground to start. I told Kate that I would sit on the clay trap and she could go the other side of a corrugated iron trap house, (so she could not shoot me) and I would fire the clays towards her over the trap house.

I sat on the trap, pulled back the strong springed arm and loaded it with a clay. Now a clay pigeon is made of coal dust compressed together to form an upturned saucer shaped disc. The trap arm is released and throws the clay at high speed up into the air where it is shot. Being made of coal dust, as soon as a shotgun pellet strikes it, it breaks into tiny bits and dust. I sat there and waited for Kate to get into position, load and call 'PULL!' which was the signal for me to release the clay.

A clay pigeon trap

A clay pigeon breaking

"PULL!" she said and thwack went the clay up into the air. I heard the shot, I saw the clay break and suddenly I felt, well, a funny feeling in my legs. I looked down and my trousers had lots of holes in them. *That's strange*, I thought, and then I saw little patches of blood around each hole. "I've been shot!" I got up and pulled my trousers down and sure enough, I had been peppered with shot. Kate was shouting, "PULL, PULL! What's the matter?" I appeared around the side of the trap house with my trousers down and said, "Kate, you've just shot me, some pellets must have ricocheted off the clay before it broke." She was shocked and devastated.

Experienced shooters tell me it's impossible to happen

We walked back to the house and Connie told me that the pellets would not have gone in very deep so she asked me to sit up on the kitchen unit, pull my trousers down and she would remove them with a pair of tweezers. I was sitting on the units and facing the kitchen door and Connie had her head buried in my crutch doing surgery, when my wife Gill walked in. All she saw was me with my trousers down and a funny look on my face, Connie with her back to her and her head in my crutch and Kate looking on. "What are you doing with my husband!" she demanded.

Needless to say, Connie's rummaging did not get the shot out as they were deep, so she phoned the doctor on duty. He told her that I should meet him at the William Julian Courtauld Hospital which was the local maternity cottage hospital. I think he thought this would be less public than the main hospital for a shotgun wound which may raise suspicions with the police. So I duly turned up and walked into a place full of women in various states of childbirth.

The doctor and the sister took me into a side room and started to gouge into my legs to see if they could extract the pellets. No anaesthetic was offered and additional pain was added to the already painful holes. At one point I made an 'Ouch!' noise and the sister said, "For heaven's sake, the women in these wards are having babies and are not making as much fuss as you – now keep quiet!"

The pellets were very deep and the doctor gave up trying to get them out, so they placed Granuflex over my legs to 'draw' them out, which didn't work except that when they were pulled off a week later by a nice nurse, it gave me a free hair removal session. OUCH! TWICE! There they are, still in my legs to this day, being picked up by the new metal detectors in airports which can detect lead.

However, with the bad luck/good luck syndrome I have, I was unlucky for the pellets to ricochet off that clay but very lucky that they did not hit me in my manhood!

Chapter 58
Can I Have a Bed for the Night?

We used to live in a seventeenth-century house in Bradford Street, Braintree and it had a coaching arch between us and the adjacent house. The front of the house was right on the pavement and opposite was a public house called The Six Bells.

One Sunday I was cleaning the car behind the archway when an elderly man shuffled up to me asking if I could put him up for the night. He looked a bit rough and the thought of telling Gill that she had to cope with a very smelly old man caused me to think of something else. So the conversation went something like this –

Me: "We can't, but the pub across the road may put you up, they have bedrooms."

Him: "Where?"

Me: "Straight across the road, there at that pub."

Him: "Where?"

Me: "If you walk straight across the road, the pub is in front of you, there, see it?"

Him: "Where?"

Me: "Straight across the road, just walk straight across the road, just straight across the road!"

Him: "I shall go straight across the road then."

Me: "Bye then and I hope you get a bed for the night there."

"Go straight on through the archway."

I went back to scraping mud off my car when I heard – Screech! BANG! And there in the road was the old man with a car stopped. I rushed out and the poor man was on the ground having had his legs broken. He looked up at me and said, "You told me to go straight across the road and I did."

Waiting for the ambulance to come I said to him, "Well at least you will have a bed for the night now."

Chapter 59
General Accidents – An Interlude
Before the Next Batch

I cannot go near a sharp or heavy implement without the strong possibility that some harm will befall me. Stanley knives, crowbars, saws, hammers, screwdrivers, anything that can harm, will harm. If I had decided to take up a profession like a butcher or a fishmonger, I would certainly be dead by now.

Gill found me one day hanging over the kitchen sink with blood pouring out of my mouth. She wondered what I had done until I pulled my thumb out of my mouth and showed her the sliced flesh, squirting blood. I had slipped with a Stanley knife when whittling a small piece of wood to place behind a hinge whilst hanging a door. I had to get a friend, Dave, to take me to hospital as I had to sit there as he drove me and clamp the open wound shut to stop the bleeding.

Asbestos is now considered a dangerous material but I can verify that it has always been like that. Whilst taking the asbestos roof off a redundant chicken house up a ladder, I was pulling the nails out with a crowbar towards me, when a stubborn nail suddenly gave way and I hit my forehead with the crowbar with some force. As I climbed down the ladder a bit wobbly, Scruffy our little dog started panicking at the amount of blood draining out of me, which intrigued me a bit as it shows how close I was to the little mutt.

A blindingly obvious way to have an accident

Without an explanation of how these things have happened you may think that I am trying to self-harm myself or commit suicide but I can assure my psychiatrist that I am not! Just because I crack my ankle bone with sledgehammer, electrocute myself whilst fiddling about with a television, fall over on lumps of broken concrete and feel faint with pain, nearly getting cut in two by flying corrugated iron (1987 hurricane) or haemorrhaging after having my tonsils out (age seven) or a tooth out (aged 30), does not mean that I intend to do it.

How to crack your ankle bone – stand on a wobbly saw bench, swing a sledgehammer and miss the post

Chapter 60
The Clock

An accident with a clock? You've got to hand it to me, if I were making up all these stories I would need to have a very vivid and weird imagination and I can assure you that I have not. But an accident with a clock...?

Gill and I decided to buy a proper clock for our mantelpiece, one that went tick-tock, so we went to Mark Marchant in Coggeshall who specialised in all types of antique clocks. After some time we chose a Regency one with a mahogany case, flowing lines and a white Roman numeral face.

We got it back home and sat it on the mantelpiece; it looked great. I decided to wind it up and Mark had explained that the springs on old clocks need very careful winding. As soon as a slightly different pressure is felt you must stop winding or the spring may snap. I was cautious and had intended to underwind the clock and I was certainly not going to overwind it.

I was winding away when suddenly the spring snapped with a loud THWANG! The large key shot out of the clock and my hand with such a force that it cut through my slipper and into my big toe. Much jumping up and down, trying to get a blood-soaked sock off and bandages ensued.

Oh! The pain of a clock key buried in one's big toe

We took it back to Mark the next day and told him the sorry tale. He informed us that some clocks did not like their new owners and did these sorts of things so they could find a better home. Sceptically we heard what the great man said and chose another old clock.

This clock was stolen along with our other antiques during our first major burglary when the unlicensed repossession people took it. I just hope it did not like its next owner!

However, an interesting question is, how did the first clock know where my big toe was…?

Chapter 61
The Tooth

We all have stories to tell about teeth and I have a few but one sticks out which may be of interest. However, if you don't like teeth stories – perhaps you should skip to the next chapter!

Because I fell over with a bottle in the face and wire up the gums at an early age, I believe that these accidents caused me to have wonky teeth. Not only that, but my teeth seem to move about the gums whenever they feel like it (I know, dentists say this is not possible but they don't have to put up with it). One day when I was about 30 I felt something protruding from the inside of my right gum. Over the next year it grew bigger and finally I went to the dentist to have it seen to.

"Oh, Mr Sarling, this is a little tooth trying to grow and has been pushed sideways by the other teeth. It will only be about an eighth of an inch long and I shall just give it a little nudge and it will pop out. Funny though, at your age your teeth should have stopped growing new ones years ago."

Gouge, crack, snip, he went for about half an hour saying things like, nasty little beggar, perhaps I should have given you some anaesthetic! Eventually, he gave up with us both in a sweat. "You'll have to go to a specialist at the hospital to get this one out; it's bigger than I thought."

So I made an appointment with St Margaret's Hospital in Epping and duly turned up in the dental department. A huge Australian man came in and he told me that he had seen the X-rays and it should not take too long to get it out as it was just a little stub of a tooth. "Yes, that's what my own dentist said," I told him.

He did at least give me some anaesthetic before he started. After a while of prodding and pulling at it, he turned to the nurse and said, "Give me that small hammer and chisel and I will tap it to loosen it." It looked like a toffee hammer and he went tap,

tap, tap but there was no movement. "Give me that bigger hammer, Nurse." Whack, whack, whack he went. I thought my jaw was going to break and still there was no movement. "Nurse, give me the large hammer and the big chisel."

I stopped him and asked, "I'm really feeling bad, can we not stop?"

And he replied, "Mr Sarling, I am nearly there, just a few more minutes and it will be out." So he went back to his stone masonry.

Now two things happened while he had his knee on my chest. I either wanted it all to end or if that was not going to happen, I wanted to go somewhere else. I am now going to tell you an experience that I have never felt before or since. I decided to faint. Yes, I decided, not involuntarily but on purpose. So I fainted, I closed my eyes and went backwards into myself and fainted.

The next thing that happened was that he was slapping me around the face to wake me up; he was also shouting at the nurse to pick herself up from the floor because she had also fainted. He shouted, "Both of you, don't you dare faint on me again, now pull yourselves together!"

Nurse, give me a bigger hammer…Nurse! Nurse!
(He would have made a good stone mason!)

Eventually, after two hours of blood sweat and tears (all three of us) he finally pulled out the one-inch curved tooth. I came out of the hospital and was taken home by Gill and a friend feeling a little bit poorly. Next day I woke up covered in blood as I had haemorrhaged in the night. I still have the hole in my gum and the tooth to this day as a memento of that lovely experience.

**My 'little' tooth compared to a one-inch wide 50 pence coin.
Feel a bit queasy, do we?**

Chapter 62
Don't Step off the Ceiling Joists!

To earn extra money, I did private construction drawings and submitted planning applications for house extensions. It was cash in the hand but I never charged much, it was just pocket money. I charged even less when I did a drawing for friends and one such project was for our friends Terry & Mary who lived in Toppesfield. They wanted to convert their roof into an extra bedroom and bathroom.

One evening Gill & I drove to their house so that I could explain the layout of the plans. While Gill and their daughter Debbie sat in the lounge, Terry, Mary and I climbed a ladder into the loft space. Before we climbed up the ladder I emphasised that they should only stand on the timber joists as we did not want anyone going through the ceiling.

We were walking about the loft and I was showing them where the partitions would be, where the dormer windows would go etc. Every now and then I would stop and reinforce my warning only to stand on the joists. We were about to finish when Mary asked me, "Mike, where is the waste pipe going?"

I turned and…and stepped between the joists! A shocked Gill & Debbie sitting on the settee suddenly saw my leg crashing through the ceiling into the lounge. A scraped leg, crushed goolies plus total embarrassment followed.

Mike! What's your leg doing in the lounge?

Chapter 63
Horses – How It All Started

In the late 1960s I was in a local ten-pin bowling team, we were called the Flintstones (original or what?). All the other teams at the Princess bowling alley hoped they would get us to compete against as it would be an easy guaranteed win for them. We were totally hopeless but it took up a Friday evening. The team consisted of my mate Dick, his girlfriend Jan and his sister Sandra.

One bowling evening the rest of my team told me that they had started horse riding and that I should have a go. Being a townie living in Dagenham I thought that the only people who had horses were either royalty or gypsies. I declined for many weeks thinking they were mad to take up such a cissy pastime.

In the end I gave in to their requests and duly turned up at a stable yard in Chigwell with not much enthusiasm. As my profession was working in mud, this did not concern me but the smell was a bit strong. They put me on this horse which had an American saddle and off we went, out of the yard and onto the main road. My only instruction was to hold on tight.

We crossed the traffic lights and went into Hainault Forest and onto a dirt track at which point all the horses stampeded. Calls were shouted back from the 'instructors' at the front like 'Don't fall off!' and 'Hang on round this corner!' and 'Mind these trees!' On we galloped for about a mile and suddenly all the horses stopped in a heap. Most riders were still on, but some must have fallen off as there were a number of empty horses.

I turned to my mates and told them that I liked this and they agreed. However, we decided that it would be a good idea if we had proper riding lessons so we went to Havering Park Riding School where the riding instructor was Rose Crawford. She taught us in a military style with classic comments thrown in such as, 'You people haven't got the brains you were born with.'

On Sundays we would ride out and one day she told me to get out Solo. He was a large white gelding, very upright and striking. Allowing me to ride him was a great honour as he was her favourite horse besides the one she rode which was a coloured horse called Cochise. However, Rose told me not to do anything stupid with him and to ride him carefully.

The routine was for all of us to ride down a small lane and into some open fields. Solo would be at the head leading and when we got to the fields, he would canter to the other end while all the other horses waited. When Solo had stopped, it was the signal for all the others to follow. We then had a breather and the herd would canter back across the field leaving Solo to be cantered back on his own with everyone else watching.

Pride comes before a fall they say and this is very true with horses. There I was watching all the lowly riders canter back with Solo standing proudly waiting his turn. As the lowlys arrived at the other end they all turned to watch me canter back sedately and I could feel Rose was watching with her eagle eyes. "OK Solo, lets show them a nice quiet canter back and they will all be so envious!" Off we went, me sitting upright, Solo cantering calmly; it felt great.

In the middle of the field was a shallow dip and as Solo got to this point with his and my head looking up, his front legs missed the ground in the dip and suddenly I was flying (again) through the air listening to Solo crashing to the ground, gasps from the lowlys and Rose going, "Oh my God, what's the idiot done now!"

I looked back at Solo getting up and he was covered in mud. The pure white horse was now black and snorting. Before I had got up and caught him, Rose had ridden up and was bellowing at me. I can't remember what she was saying but again my mother was apparently accused of not being married etc. I think she forgave me as I was allowed to ride him on other occasions but with a, 'Don't effing well do what you did last time etc.'

The not-so-sure-footed Solo…

After a while my three partners suggested that we bought our own horse each having a 25% share in it. We duly purchased Kerry from John Holliwell a noted horse dealer near Brentwood. Kerry was a dear horse but required a large amount of encouragement to go. However, she was very safe for us four novices.

Within a month Dick & Jan decided to get married and because they needed money they asked Sandra and me if we could buy out their two shares, which we did. It was only a few months later that Sandra asked if I would buy her share and suddenly I was in possession of a whole horse. Within the space of six months I had gone from not knowing what a horse was to owning one.

I understand from my then future wife Gill that I turned up at the stable yard and pompously announced that I owned a horse to which she replied, "So what? I have four."

Gill and my relationship was fraught at the beginning to the point that one day I made some comment to her and she threw a can of hoof oil at me. Rather that step sideways, I ducked into its path and I still have the lump on my forehead today. The second time she tried to kill me was when she suggested that I go riding with her and her friend Pauline. Out we went with me at the rear on slow Kerry, when they started to canter through a wood. Kerry decided that this was great fun weaving in and out of the trees until she cut a corner and the gap between the saddle and a tree was two inches and the width of my leg was four inches. Result – smashed knee, blood, bandages and a new pair of jodhpurs.

Chapter 64
The Horsebox

When I first met Gill she had a Land Rover and horse trailer and she got other people to drive it as she does not drive. One day she decided to change them for a proper horsebox. This was a 1950 Bedford O Type like this one…

**3.5-litre, six-cylinder engine,
a flat battery and a starting handle**

Always trying to impress her after the hoof oil can incident? She came to me one day and said, "Your company has lorries, don't they? Can you drive them?"

"Of course I can," I said (lying).

"Oh good," she said, "you can drive my new horsebox to the horse shows!"

The day it arrived in the yard, my heart sank at the thought of little me driving the great big brute. It used to stand idle all week so by each weekend the battery was always flat so starting it was a ritual. I used to get to the stables early as did Gill. She got the horses ready for the show while I started the lorry.

Instructions for starting a 1950 Bedford with a flat battery – Lift both the side bonnets, tie them up so they don't crash down on your head, remove the distributor cap and wipe it clean of any moisture, remove five of the spark plugs (the sixth one was inaccessible), spray quick start into each cylinder ensuring you get each spark plug back in each hole before it evaporates, re-fit the spark leads, turn on the ignition, place the starting handle into the front shaft and swing it hard ensuring that the 3.5-litre engine does not kick back and throw you on the ground or worse, break your arm!

After swinging over the huge six-cylinder engine for five minutes, collapse in a heap and sit on the bumper to recover. Repeat the whole exercise two or three more times until it starts. Of course, sometimes it did kick back and laid me on the ground. Gill would often come over and say, "Haven't you got that started yet, we're going to be late!"

Instructions for driving a 1950 Bedford – No power steering, huge steering wheel, spongy brakes, crash gearbox (double de-clutch on all gears) and you can't hear yourself think level of noise – plus a load full of live horses in the back! I only relaxed when we got it back to the stables after the shows.

Instructions for double clutching – Whilst on the move, release the throttle until the revs die down, the clutch pedal is then pressed, and the gearbox lever is shifted into neutral, the clutch pedal is then released, the driver matches the engine RPM to the gear RPM either using the throttle (when changing up) or waiting for RPM to decrease (when changing down) until they are at a level suitable for shifting into the next gear, at the moment when the revs between engine and gear are closely matched, the driver then instantly presses the clutch again to shift into the next gear. The result should be a very smooth gear change if you get it right and a loud crunching sound if you get it wrong.

I drove that vehicle for a number of years until after we were married when one day it needed some new tyres and an exhaust box and as these were going to cost £100 which was a fortune for us, it had to go. The horsebox would be worth a lot of money now.

I must tell you a funny little story about the lorry. One day we were coming back from a horse show when I pulled into a garage to fill up with petrol. In those days an attendant would come out and fill up the tank. On the Bedford the tank was just below the floor of the horsebox, so the horses were standing above the tank.

This attendant was filling up the tank when our New Forest pony, Robin, decided to have a pee. Suddenly the guy stood back and shouted to me, "Come here I think you have a leak in your fuel tank – look at this!" His arm was dripping in urine as the liquid was pouring through the floorboards and over the tank and onto the ground.

I said, "My word your right!" and quickly put the tank cap back on and told him I would get it fixed. I quickly paid him and drove off.

The poor man did not twig that the 'leak' was coming from above and not below. I wonder if he smelt his arm afterwards and thought, *That's a strange petrol smell.*

Chapter 65
The Horsebox and the Stallion

Rose (Solo's owner, chapter 63) ran the riding school where I kept my horse. She was a small, unmarried lady who called a spade a bloody great shovel, if you know what I mean. She used to file her fingernails on the brick wall whilst talking to you. During her riding lessons you would always hear her shouting, "You bloody people don't know a bloody thing, now sit up and kick on!" She was a great character, one of those wonderful people you meet so rarely who is and tries to be different – eccentric we call it!

One day Rose asked Gill if I would transport a mare to a stallion from the yard in Havering to Stock about 20 miles away in her horsebox. Gill of course offered my services without asking me but it was a simple job, just take a mare to a stallion and leave it there for a week to be covered. "No problem, Rose," she said.

It was a dark evening but luckily, the Bedford started after only two spark plug removal attempts and I drove it out of our remote stable yard and across the road into the main block. I backed it into the yard and pulled down the ramp and prepared the straw on the floor and waited for Rose to get the mare with the engine still running as it may not have started again.

There were the usual little horsey kids running around the place so I did not take much notice of them. Rose then walked up and gave me the following instructions:

- ✓ "Do you mind if the kids come with us, good that's settled, get in kids!" And they all piled into the box and the cab. "OK, Rose!"
- ✓ "The mare hates horseboxes and once she is in, you must not stop for anything otherwise she will kick the horsebox to bits, is that clear?"

✓ "Yes Rose!!"
✓ "Drive slowly and carefully all the way."
✓ "Yes Rose!"

"But, but, but!" I mumbled. "Right Mike, as soon as I get the mare inside, Fred here will close the ramp and then you just drive – don't stop!"

I got into position with the lorry in gear, heard the crashing hooves going up the ramp, the snorting horse, the ramp being slammed shut and Rose shouting, "DRIVE, MIKE!" as she leaped aboard the lorry. Off I went out of the yard and onto the road, slowly driving and estimating traffic, bends, roundabouts and other things that might cause me to stop at any time. Traffic lights were particularly tricky and I had to slowly creep it forward until the green light came on and then off we would go again at 20 mph. Long traffic queues built up behind us but the thought of the box being smashed up because I stopped to let them pass greatly concerned me, especially about what Gill would say who was in the back with the kids.

I must say I did extremely well and did not stop for one second. As we drove into the stable yard at Stock the thought suddenly occurred to me that I would actually have to stop when I got there. I mentioned this to Rose, "What happens when I stop in the yard?"

Rose said, "We had better be quick getting the ramp down then!" Needless to say it took me at least 5 seconds to stop the lorry, jump out, get the ramp down and open the gates at which point the mare went berserk! She lashed out at the gates just missing my hands with her rear foot which went through the gap breaking one of the wooden slats.

She came crashing down the ramp onto the concrete yard with Rose now in tow, shaking. All the little kids tumbled out of the lorry from every corner and I realised there was about a dozen of them, all talking loudly and excited. The stallion owner came up to us and took one look at the mare's cut fetlock and said these words. "She's not going to support the stallion on that rear foot tomorrow, we shall have to cover her now. Is she ready, Rose?" at which point Rose said she was definitely ready.

Now I was 22 years old and had had some dealings with sexual matters but I was very naïve about many aspects of the subject. I had never seen a mare covered by a stallion before but my mind started whirling around about what was going to happen in this floodlit square yard. Then suddenly, I realised that there were a dozen kids with goggle eyes all waiting for the performance to start! I mumbled something like, "Rose, do you think I should take these kids back to the horsebox until it is over?" for her to reply, "Na! It'll increase their education – it's all natural."

The children loved it!

I stood there totally embarrassed with a scarlet face as the snorting stallion pranced forward in the glare of the lights surrounded by kids, leaping onto the back of the mare with the handlers giving the stallion a helping hand with accuracy! Oh My God, the grunting and the grinding, the smiling faces of the little kids, the stupid look on the face of the crazy mare and the enormous size of the – well the – the todger thing. Was I the only one there who was embarrassed? You bet yer!

Chapter 66
Granite

After we were married, Gill's sister Beth and I thought that we needed some proper lessons to hone up on our riding skills. We decided to go to a good school in Epping which was about 20 miles away from my home in Brentwood. Beth and I arrived at the school one evening and I was asked by the instructor to use a horse called Granite and to get him out of his stable.

I got to his stable and he turned out to be a very large grey gelding all saddled up and ready to go. Outside the stable door was a sloping concrete ramp and as I led him out at the top of the ramp, he stood on my left foot with his dinner plate size shoe. He obviously thought the ground was moving so he clamped the foot down as we slid down the slope. Whimpering with pain, I finally pushed him off my foot and got on using a mounting block.

Half a ton of Granite on my toe

My foot was thumping with pain but we carried on with the one-hour riding lesson without me telling anyone about the incident and acting normal. I then had to drive home and I decided that I would keep my riding boots on rather than look at the mess inside. As it was my left foot, using the clutch was murder. I got home and Gill was in bed. She heard some peculiar noises coming from downstairs and came down to investigate.

She found me trying to get my left boot off and asked me what had happened. I lay on the settee and she pulled the boot off with me stifling a scream. As she pealed the bloody sock off, the mashed big toe was revealed.

I always try to look on the bright side and assumed that I would go to work as normal the next day, but Gill decided that I needed hospital treatment. She walked down the road to my old company Cawoods who had an office close by and asked Stewart, the guy who took over from me when I left but after Robert (of flash bang wallop fame) had left, to take me to hospital, which he did, where the nice nurse carefully took the nail off my big toe with a squelch.

Chapter 67
General Riding Accidents

I don't intend to explain all my riding accidents, incidents and adventures for two reasons. Firstly, anyone who has been around horses for any length of time would have had just as many as me, I am sure. Secondly, the number of events I have had would end up boring you silly. I will only explain the unusual ones that may or may not have happened to other people.

Besides many cuts, bruises, crunches, sprains, bites and others, my incidents include:

- ✓ Being dragged through a thick hedge where there was no gap when riding Melba just because someone started sweeping a farmyard I was passing at the time.
- ✓ Being run away with Robin when he bolted and then the metal stirrup broke.
- ✓ Jumping onto a grassy bank whilst riding Robin which turned out to be semi-liquid manure clamp and as he sunk in about three foot deep, I jumped off and also sunk. We both stunk like skunks.

Splashing about in a dung heap

- ✓ Being dragged downhill while leading Gina at high speed, letting go and not being able to stop myself running so I purposely tripped myself up, ending up with a face full of mud.
- ✓ Burning my hands when ropes are pulled through, bashing heads on overhead branches, bending back fingers and generally falling off.

Falling off a horse is an interesting concept. Imagine you are sitting on a wall five foot high and someone suddenly pushes you either backwards or forwards off the wall. The ground could be anything from wet soft mud to hard concrete. Imagine that you add some momentum to that push and then imagine how you are going to hit the ground. It's going to hurt whatever happens – isn't it? What limb will you put out to save yourself and then get damaged?

That's what it is like falling off a horse. Why do people ride horses? I dunno!

My accident list with horses goes on but in all the 30 odd years I rode, I never broke a bone. I crunched, cracked and disjointed them, yes, but never broke one. I put this down to all the milk I have drunk all my life which must have made my bones strong and I must say I have really tried to break them in many different ways.

Chapter 68
Honey

Honey was a lovely horse, usually calm and serene she sometimes gave me a surprise. One day Gill and I went on a 20-mile long-distance ride which had jumps along the route. After about half a mile we came to our first jump and Honey went towards it full of enthusiasm. As she took off, she suddenly decided that she would not jump it and spun around almost in mid-air. I had no chance of staying on and flew through the air backwards and landed on an upright post with my coccyx (that's the base of your spine).

Although I was in a bit of pain, I decided that Honey was not going to be disobedient like that so I told Gill that I would not only continue to ride the 20 miles but do all the jumps as well. Honey performed perfectly, flowing over all the jumps. However, as we arrived back at the start, I could not get off the horse, I was rigid with pain. Eventually, with the help of some friends, they got me off and drove me home. I was laid up for a few weeks with a cracked spine and then afterwards I got to work by crawling up to my car and pulling myself up into the driver's seat. To get out I rolled over onto the ground and then pulled myself up the door. The pain stayed with me for many years with me wincing every time I stood on uneven ground. That's what one has to put up with when dealing with horses!

Honey also pulled our trap and although she did it very well, Gill's driving had something to be desired. Apparently, she assumed that if she was on the road, all other road users should get off it! There were a few occasions when I bailed out the back in fear. Looking at a pony and trap, you may think how serene it looks – wrong!

One day the livery yard held a fancy dress competition and Gill dressed me up as a gnome. Tall pointy red hat, green smock and yellow tights with pointy shoes. I was also given a whip which looked like a fishing rod. Honey was done up like a garden covered in petals and as I came out of the yard and into the arena, everyone laughed and told me I fitted the part completely – I hate gnomes!

I want to go Gnome

Chapter 69
Sherry

Sherry was the best person in the whole world. We first met her when she took over the stables near Braintree where we kept our four horses. She was happy-go-lucky and was friends with everyone she met. She was the person with the broken wrist during the snow incident. The late Sherry will not mind me saying that she was on the large side. One day she asked me if I would collect two young ponies from a field near Finchingfield, so I hooked up our trailer and took her together with my wife Gill and her sister Beth to help out.

At the time, we had a horse/trap trailer which had a solid partition running across the width rather than down the centre as in a normal horse trailer. The horses went in the front and the trap in the back with the shafts sticking out of the opening.

We arrived at the field and while Beth and Sherry caught the ponies, Gill and I prepared the trailer. The ponies were not trailer trained and we had a bit of a problem getting them in. I waggled a bucket of food over the partition while Gill closed the ramp as soon as they were in. As the ramp shut behind the little beasts, they went berserk and started kicking and rushing about.

"Beth!" I said, "Give me your arms and I will pull you over the partition." Beth weighs about seven stone and with a jump she was on top of the partition and I pulled her to safety. "Sherry, you next," I shouted.

"I'm too heavy for you, Mike," she said.

Time was short before she was damaged, so I shouted, "No you're not, give me your arms," and with all my strength, I pulled her up and onto the partition, at which point we both over toppled and she came crashing down on me. I was enveloped by my friend who took all the wind out of me.

I'm sure Sherry had a crush on me

About a week later I went to the doctor's complaining of chest pains. He checked me over and asked if I had banged my chest because he suspected that I could have cracked ribs. I told him that the only thing I could think of was that a large lady friend of mine had landed on top of me from a great height. At this point he raised his eyebrows with a look of, 'I don't want to know about your sexual deviations, thank you.'

I was working on construction of the M25 motorway at the time, about 35 miles away and my Land Rover was not a comfortable vehicle when you have cracked ribs. I used to drive a few miles to another chap who also worked on the road project and then he would drive me into work whilst I held my arms across my chest holding the ribs in place. Where there's a will, there's a way.

Chapter 70
Purdy

I bought Purdy from our friend Jane as she had difficulty controlling her. She was a dark bay thoroughbred but like me, she was a runt standing at only 14.3 hands, only one inch bigger than a pony. After a few miscommunications, we hit it off and she turned out to be the best little horse I could ever want. She was either brave or stupid as she would go over, through or under any obstacle I put her to. We both had a lot of fun together.

One of my hacks out was to go across the road from our stables and round the local sewage works settling beds. These were reed beds intersected by grass banks which one could ride around. The water would filter through the beds and then outlet into the River Blackwater. One day we came up to the sewage farm entrance only to find it shut off for some construction work.

A few weeks later we went there again and it was open, so we trotted and cantered around the banks. As we came up to the last bank, I noticed a new manhole had been constructed in the middle. I could see that it had been backfilled but it all looked Ok to ride over. As Purdy stepped near the manhole, both her front legs dropped straight down into the wet mud backfill. Her chest hit the ground hard and she smacked her mouth on the manhole cover. Needless to say, not to be outdone, I went over her head and smacked my face on the manhole cover as well.

Collecting impressions of manhole covers – by not using the brass rubbing method

I struggled to get up as Purdy splashed about in the wet mud. Eventually, I was able to help her up out of the mire and we both stood there thinking, "Woz 'appened?" Then the competition started – who was producing the most blood. Poor Purdy won, I'm afraid. We walked back into our yard for Gill to look up and see two dejected objects, covered in mud and blood.

Chapter 71
Hunting

That's an evocative and emotional word to lots of people. It brings with it so many emotions that I will not even go anywhere near it except to say that I went fox hunting a number of times during my 30 odd years riding. I also witnessed the death of an activity which had been in existence since the beginning of time on earth. Hunting is now carried out by the hounds chasing a human being dragging a scented rag.

The late John O'Shea, huntsman to the East Essex Foxhounds

On the occasions that I did partake of the sport, I had some interesting events which may not have happened to other hunters. Just about everyone who rides in the hunting field has had many accidents, incidents and adventures, but of course I also had unusual ones as well. First of all though, I would like to take you through one of my typical hunting days to give the reader who has never experienced such an event, a taste of what it was like over the next few chapters.

I must say that during my time of hunting, shooting and fishing, my attitude was very different to my attitude now. I was pursuing country sports with country people and not giving much thought as to the actual animals we were exploiting.

I am very lucky to own a large field behind my house and we are surrounded by set aside fields of grass. Over the past few years since we have not had horses, a lot of wildlife now comes into our paddock and it is great to observe these creatures and their habits.

The fox is always thought to be the nasty villain but we have badgers that come into our garden and a wild cat and the foxes are very wary of both. And when I see pheasants with chicks and how they attend them and the way rabbits play together, I wonder how I could have willingly shot or hunted them.

I now think that chasing a human dragging a scented rag with foxhounds and shooting clay pigeons is for me but I still respect the ways of the country sportsmen and women.

Chapter 72
A Typical Hunting Day

Some rich or retired people hunted two or three days a week but I only managed two days a month if I was lucky due to work commitments and the lack of money. My hunting days were therefore very special to me. I would come home from work on a Thursday and if Gill had not finished dealing with the horses, I would give her a hand. I would then exercise the horse that I was taking hunting, usually Purdy. This was all carried out in the dark under a few small floodlights, as hunting took place in the winter months between October and March. After exercise, I would get the horse trailer ready and then go in for a late dinner.

Friday evening would see me cleaning firstly the horse and then my tack and boots, laying out my clothes and getting my sandwich and hip flask ready. The horse, tack and clothing had to be absolutely spick and span with the black boots polished to a mirror finish. This was for two reasons, firstly it is a great insult to the Hunt Masters and our hosts for anyone not presenting themselves in a perfect condition but more importantly, Gill the Hunt Secretary would usually examine everyone like a military inspection and make comments and give you a look which told you seriously off. She would say something like, "Michael! The sole of one of your boots has dung on it!"

"Sorry Gill, I must have stepped in it when I mounted, I shall get it cleaned."

Then the great day would dawn early. I would go down to the horses and feed them and find that Purdy had somehow removed her rug in the night and she had decided that her own dung would be nice to roll in and her tail would be matted with wood chips from her bedding.

Eventually, I would arrive at the meet, all spick and span and mount up. After a few sausage rolls and a drink we would move off and because Purdy and I were usually the smallest

189

combination, we would be plastered from head to foot in mud within 5 minutes. All that preparation work gone in a flash.

After that we would gallop across fields, trot fast down roads, jump fences, scrabble up and down deep ditches, crash through hedges and generally have a very exciting time intermingled with standing around in the cold and taking to the hip flask amongst the sweaty steam coming off the hot horses.

Purdy and me at the meet before being plastered in mud

By the time Purdy and I usually arrived back home in the dark and we were usually exhausted, cold, wet and hungry. I would spend the first hour cleaning down Purdy ensuring that she had no cuts or scrapes and giving her a hot bran mash tea. After this I would go into the house and smell the stew that Gill had prepared, pull off all my clothes and get into a warm bath with a glass of whisky. Then I would come down in my dressing gown and eat the hot stew with another whisky.

At that point I always had the best feeling in the world. After all the preparation in getting the horse and all the equipment ready and then the rigors of the day, the exhausted and relaxed calm that I felt could not be recreated by any other means, other than by banging your head against a wall and then stopping!

Chapter 73
Purdy's Puncture

One day the opening meet of the East Essex Foxhounds was only about four miles from my home so I decided to hack there and not use the horse trailer. I had a great day's hunting from Bovington Hall over to Finchingfield, Wethersfield and then across to Gosfield returning to Bovington Hall, a ride of about 30 miles. On this occasion it was not muddy and Purdy and I were not too plastered. I was near home, coming back across some fields when Purdy's head bobbed a bit more than usual. I studied this for a few more strides and thought she may be a bit lame. I got off and inspected her legs scraping away some loose mud. I could not find anything amiss so I trotted her up and again I could not detect any lameness. She looked bright and happy so I remounted and rode home. Cleaning her off was easy and I settled her down to her warm mash tea, rugged her up, tied up the hay net and made sure she was happy.

About 8 o'clock I went back down the stables to check on her and the other horses but when I came to her stable she was in the corner looking miserable with her hind leg tucked up and off the ground. She would only move by hopping about on three legs. Something was seriously wrong as Purdy was not a horse to worry about pain as she and I had been in a lot of scrapes together and she never complained. This time was different. I called Gill and she thought that she had cracked a bone in her leg, so we called the vet.

The vet gave her an examination and after a long and detailed search found a small puncture wound in the heel of her leg. I was only about 15mm wide but went in deep. After further examination, he found that it had partly severed the tendon and this had caused the reaction to pull up her leg. She was unable to put it to the ground even if she wanted to. We assumed that she had trodden on a sharp flint which ran upwards into her. Flints that are split can be as sharp as a razor and were used as tools by Stone Age man. The soil around Braintree is flint country and it is amazing that more accidents like this do not happen.

The reason for this story is not so much the accident with Purdy and more about human nature. The vet bandaged up Purdy's leg very tightly and told me that she should be box rested. She should also be kept very quiet and still because if she moved suddenly, she may well tear the final part of the tendon and would then have to be put down. He also explained that if it was going to heal it would take about six weeks, so keeping a fit animal still for this length of time while seeing all her mates being let out into the paddock every day would be difficult.

Behind our stables is a farm and the field immediately behind contained stubble. I had noticed that being near Guy Fawkes Night, some local residents had got permission from the farmer to build a bonfire about 20 feet away from our stables. It suddenly occurred to me that all the noise of the fire and fireworks not to mention the noise from the children may cause the horses to panic and rush about their stables. I decided to go out and ask the people if they could move the bonfire further away from the stables. I gathered them together and explained what had happened to Purdy and what would happen if she caused the tendon to break. I also offered to help them move the bonfire further away.

What reaction did I get? 'Well you shouldn't have gone hunting then!' 'Serves you right if she has to be put down,' and things like 'Our children's fun is more important than your horse.' 'We don't see any reason why we need to move it.'

I could not believe the callous and selfish nature of their comments and I then got angry. I reacted by telling them that they were FB's and that I shall let them know when she has to be put down so they could all come and gloat as she is shot! This produced no reaction from them and they continued to build the bonfire so that it was higher than our stables – I think on purpose.

A few days later, they had their party. I stood with Purdy in her stable, stroking her and keeping her calm throughout the flashes, bangs, wizzes etc. We could even feel the heat of the fire through the brick walls and I had to also check on our hay store to make sure that sparks did not set it alight.

After an hour of this, all the happy noisy people went home and left the fire to die down. It was midnight before I could be certain that the embers were not going to spread through the stubble and onto my property or cause a spark. Throughout the whole evening, Purdy and the rest of the horses were as good as gold and I feel that they all knew the importance of keeping calm for Purdy's sake.

The next day I went to see the farmer and explained the whole sorry tale and never again did he allow those nice people to have a bonfire on his land again.

Chapter 74
Trinity and the Dog Rose

Trinity was a lovely dapple-grey Connemara pony that Gill purchased from a small island off the Welsh coast called Bardsey Island. Trinity turned out to have a sense of humour which did not always accord with the humans around her. Apparently, she used to chase the sheep on the island over the cliffs to their deaths and the owners decided to sell her to Gill.

Trinity looking sweet – I've not been thrown off yet!

She had an amazing ability to suddenly move in such a way as to throw you off onto the ground in a split second and then stand and smile at you. She loved doing things which were exciting and hunting was one of them. One day we were hunting at Beazley End and I was sitting on Trinity on the road watching the hounds work in the field the other side of a hedge. They could not find any scent so John the huntsman gave up and collected all the hounds together and made their way out of the field and onto the road.

One of the things you must always do with hounds, especially if your horse is unpredictable, is to turn the head of your horse to face the hounds as they go past. This way, your horse cannot kick the hounds (except with its front legs if it is that way inclined!) So as the hounds went past followed by the huntsman and the rest of the field (all the other riders) I turned Trinity to face the hounds. As I did so her back legs went down a ditch and she reared up tossing me into a Dog Rose bush.

There I was, laying on my back five foot off the ground, legs in the air surrounded by sharp thorns with the huntsman and all the field laughing fit to burst. Some of the more elderly lady riders later admitted that they may have wet themselves.

A rose between one thousand thorns?

I could not move but luckily a number of foot followers gradually pulled away the spiky branches and lowered me to the ground. This took longer than it should have due to them all laughing. In the meantime I am sure Trinity was also laughing. Eventually I got back on her and trotted back to the rest of the field where they were all still laughing, so I asked some of the ladies if they would be kind enough to pull out the spiky bits from my backside.

Chapter 75
Bertie

One day my friend Connie asked me if I wanted to take Bertie her Cob, hunting. He was a short stocky little bay horse and was known to be a brave lad. His only problem was that he was not keen on horse trailers and would sometimes be a bit of a problem going in. The day came and Bertie loaded up Ok and I arrived at the meet about five miles away. In hindsight, I should have hacked to the meet instead of transporting him there, but hindsight is a great thing – what!

It was a great hunting day and we all arrived back at the farmyard where our trailers were parked, exhausted. I decided that as Bertie was now tired he may just go straight in the trailer without a fuss so I left all the tack on him and led him up the ramp. I asked a friend if he could close the ramp as soon as Bertie was in and he just walked up the ramp following me in front, no bother at all. Just as my mate was going to lift the ramp, Bertie pulled back from me and shot down the ramp backwards. He immediately galloped out of the farmyard and into the road heading for home with reins and stirrups flailing about around him. My reaction was to run after him in full hunting kit, long boots and all. Bertie was trotting along quite happily but my thoughts turned to the major road he would have to cross before he got home and the thought of a loose horse careering across the traffic filled me with dread. I quickened my running.

A Land Rover and trailer came up the side of me and slowed down and stopped. It was Anna and she said, "Want a lift, Mike?" I jumped in, slammed the door and she drove off. After a little while I said,

"Anna, can't you go a bit faster?"

And she said, "Why, are you in a hurry to get home?"

I was getting a bit fractious and said, "No! Anna, I'm chasing Bertie, Connie's horse, he got away from me and I'm trying to catch him before he goes across the A131 at Great Leighs!"

"Oh Mike, I had better speed up then," so she put her foot down and raced down the road towards Bertie. He came into view still trotting happily along on the left side of the road. We slowly gained on him and as we came level I asked Anna to cut him off at a road junction. I was out of the door before she stopped and grabbed his reins. All was calm until Anna said, "Oh my God, we've been whizzing along and around bends and my horse is in the trailer. I hope he is alright?" Luckily he was and I climbed back onto Bertie and rode him back to my trailer.

Faster Anna, faster!

Chapter 76
Judging Horses

My wife Gill used to judge horses and ponies at local shows and sometimes she used me as her steward. I would always put in my two pennyworth of advice when she was doing her final line up, often when it wasn't wanted. Sometimes she would ask me to ride judge whilst she did the conformation judging.

The judging class would go as follows. All the entrants would ride into the ring and be studied by both of us. They would then be asked to walk, trot and canter on both reins. Once they were stopped, we would concur and pull in our initial line up in order of quality. I would then ride each horse in turn and once ridden, Gill would have the saddle taken off and the rider would stand the horse and trot it up while she studied the conformation. After all the horses had been judged we would both discuss each ones best and worst points and then jointly decide the prize order.

We were judging at the Felsted Horse Show one June day and the ground was as hard as concrete. I had recently bought a new riding hat which had cost me £150 and it had all the latest safety features on it. Little did I know I would need it that day. It was a lovely summer's day and Gill and I had judged about three classes when the next class came into the ring. When ride judging I would have someone to throw me up on each horse as it was quite an effort to keep mounting dozens of horses from the ground. I would crook my left leg and my helper would grab it and say one, two, three and at the same time as he threw me up, I would jump from my right leg and quietly settle into the saddle and at the same time gather up the reins which were usually double (four reins).

I got to the next horse in line which was in about sixth place and was just about to mount when I recognised the rider who was holding the horses' head. I stopped and said, "Weren't you the pair last year that when I went to mount, your horse bolted knocking you to the ground and leaving me to land on my feet?"

"Ah yes," she said, "we have been training him all year not to do that, so he is alright now?" I looked at her with a few doubts but she had paid her entry money and I was the ride judge so I had to give her horse a fair chance.

I got hold of the reins and crooked my leg to be thrown up, grabbed the rear of the saddle and – one, two, three jump and I rose up in the air and landed as gently as I could into the saddle. Sure enough, the horse stood there but as I went to gather up the reins he suddenly bolted, knocking over the rider and her assistant. It went so fast that I went over backwards and flew off the tail end of the mad animal.

I have been thrown off horses a great number of times and as I'm in mid-air I usually have time to think 'Oh blast, this is going to hurt and there is nothing I can do about it.' On this occasion I did not even have time to consider my fate. I hit the ground flat on my back hitting my head at the same time. There was a loud CRACK! I sat up winded and my first thought was that I had damaged my new riding hat, so I took it off and pressed the sides. It was not broken at all, so I put it back on and got up. The mad horse was still being chased around the ring by its owner as I approached the next horse in line. It was being held by a man who said, "Are you OK? That was a terrible fall." I told him that I was fine and would be continuing the class. I proceeded to ride the remaining six horses in walk, trot and canter and Gill and I completed the class and gave out the prizes.

Something went 'CRACK!'

199

The next class came in and I was thrown up onto the first horse, a very big bay mare. I walked her around the ring, went into a trot and then a canter. On the first few canter strides my neck hurt and I felt very strange. The pain was so bad that I had to stop and I walked the horse up to Gill. I told her my neck really hurt and I didn't think I could ride any more horses.

The next day I was sitting in my office when I convinced myself that I had broken my neck as the pain was getting worse, so I went off to Broomfield Hospital for an X-Ray. The doctor was dismissive of a broken neck and after some X-Rays they came back and told me that I had probably just strained a few muscles and to wear a collar for a few days. They also told me not to drive with a collar on so as I got back into my car and I took off the collar to drive home.

Some years later when I was learning to fly, Brian, my instructor told me that I should keep turning around to look out for other aircraft. As my neck had become very stiff, I could not do as he asked and he told me to get my neck sorted out by a chiropractor. Off I went and the first thing they did was X-Ray my neck. As the consultant came back into the room he said, "Mr Sarling, when did you damage your neck, you have three crushed vertebrae that have fused together, that's why you have a stiff neck?" What stopped me from dying on that June day I shall never know but it will be one of my questions when I meet my guardian angel.

Chapter 77
Saffy

Around the year 2002 we lost our last horses to old age and I decided not to ride anymore. After about six months, I grew restless for another horse and had a few bad experiences whilst trying out some very dubious ones for sale. In the end I bought a 16.2 bay Hanoverian mare called Saffron Bay Lady or Saffy. She turned out to be very athletic but a bit unpredictable. She caused both Gill and I quite a bit of bodily damage during her time with us and I came off her a number of times.

Saffy looking shiny and me looking scruffy

As she had the potential to be a good show jumper, I booked up a course of lessons from a well-known trainer at Towerlands, a local equestrian centre. I was about halfway through our training when I was practicing at home and we went over a fence with Saffy over jumping it rather high. To stop myself tipping forward over her neck on landing, I put my right hand onto her neck. As she landed with a jolt, most of my fingers went left on her neck and my little finger went right with a crack. I assumed that I had successfully cracked the bones at the base of my finger which was quite painful.

My next lesson was a few days later, so I bandaged up my hand real tight and put on a leather glove. This held all the bones together and it felt Ok. The lesson was going well and the trainer had got all the class going over some pretty big single fences. He then told us all that he now wanted us to go around the whole course as if we were competing. We had jumped over them all with no problem, all we had to do was to jump them in a sequence. I was about the third one to go and Saffy was jumping them with feet to spare. As we came round a corner to take one of the easier fences, she went to jump and then stopped dead and at the same time swung around. I flew through the air and landed amongst the poles…on my right hand! Cor! That hurt a lot.

Saffy would be an angel for ages and then suddenly she would explode, usually chucking me off with painful consequences. One day I decided to hack out across the road down a bridle path whilst Gill took our little dog Scruffy for a walk along the same path. I turned a corner and heard some scramble motorbikes at the far end of the path, so I went through a hedge into a field of rough grass to keep out of their way. Just as I was walking in the field, one of the bikes roared down the path at high speed and as he got level with me changed gear with a loud crash. Saffy by this time was prancing about but with the added crash she bucked so high that I was propelled up into the air. I had time to think, 'Oh, this is going to hurt' when I landed flat on my back again. There is one large stone in that field, I have checked this out since the accident, yes only one and I landed on it, crunch! Unbeknown to me I had cracked my scapular bone in my shoulder and was winded. I lay there looking up at the sky amongst the tall grass unable to move.

Gill had gone a slightly different route and had come into the same field when she saw in the distance a horse happily eating grass but with a saddle and bridle on. *That's strange* she thought, *It looks just like Saffy,* as she approached it she realised it was Saffy but where was I? Saffy came up to her and she looked around to see where I had fallen off. Suddenly she noticed a shape trying to get up off the ground. I had rolled over on my front and slowly managed to get one arm and then the next to push myself up into an 'on all fours' position.

She walked up to me leading Saffy and Scruffy by which time I was on my feet feeling very painful. "Come on," she said, "get back on and I shall lead you home." We went around the field to where the motorcyclists were gathered and as she got up to them she tore them all off a strip telling them what they had done to her husband and how irresponsible they all were etc. I don't know about them but she terrified the life out of me!

Chapter 78
Saffy and the Puma

There have been many reports of large cats being seen in the countryside and some have been reported around the Braintree area. Most of these have been proved to be nothing more than a large pussycat or a dog. But after a policewoman reported seeing what see thought was a Puma north of the town, I was out riding Saffy and we had an experience.

Saffy often got frightened by a plastic bag, a white sign or some other such 'fearful' object when we rode out and it usually ended up with her bucking me off. In this way she altered my physical appearance a number of times. However, this particular day we were riding along a bridleway next to a thick wood north of Stisted when Saffy suddenly slowed up when something rustled in the undergrowth in the wood. I saw the bushes moving but then Saffy stopped and all her hairs stood on end. Her head went up and she started trembling; she would not move.

The poor animal was literally terrified and rather than doing her usual thing of chucking me off and galloping away, she started to slowly creep forward as if on stilts, peering into the wood. I could not make out anything but she could obviously smell something. To this day I really don't know if there was a Puma in the wood but on the other hand I have never known a horse to be so terrified. Mystery unsolved.

Chapter 79
Saffy's Colic

It was always a traumatic time when we had to put down our horses but we always knew when the time was right. We never let them suffer just because of our feelings; ending their suffering always came first.

Although Saffy caused me a lot of physical pain and injury I still felt a lot of affection for her. One day Gill and I were out all day and our neighbour Bob was looking after his horses and Saffy and he phoned me while I was driving back in the evening when I was about an hour away. He explained that Saffy had contracted colic and he had called the vet who had said that it was so bad that she had to be put down straight away. My mind was spinning around and I asked to speak to the vet. He explained that Saffy's colic was very serious and she was in great pain, he had given her some painkillers but that it could not go on any longer.

I asked him if he could wait until I got back and he advised me that she may have died by then, so he needed my permission to put her down there and then. I asked him for a few minutes to think about it and I would phone him back. Gill and I discussed what we should do and it was agony driving and thinking. I made a decision and phoned the vet back. I told him that he should not put her down and to give her some more painkillers and asked him if he would he come back in a few hours so we could discuss how to proceed.

We arrived home and saw Bob and walked down to the stables. There was Saffy standing with her head down, sweating and looking very poorly, it was a pitiful sight. The vet came back and advised me that Saffy had obviously got something stuck in her gut and the pain would get worse until the gut produced toxins which would then kill her. However, we agreed that because he was on duty all night he was prepared to leave it and for me to phone him as soon as I decided to put her down. He reminded me not to allow her to lay down and roll over as this would twist her gut and she would die quickly.

I know what he was thinking and it was that I was only thinking of myself and not the horse. This was not true as I had a sixth sense that she would recover. By this time I had learnt to trust what my guardian angel told me and not my own mind. It had taken me 50 years to trust her/him and that's what I did then. I got a chair and put it in the corner of Saffy's stable and sat down. To allow the other horses to sleep and to relax Saffy I turned the lights out and settled down to watch her.

Saffy's breathing was low and laboured and it was agony for me to sit there and watch the life slowly going out of her. At about midnight I stood next to her and laid my hands on her. Now we are going into the weird world of healing. I discovered many years ago that if someone had a pain and I laid my hands on the area, the pain would disappear. I have done this for many people and even myself and it seems to work. There are a number of things that could be happening with this 'gift' that I seem to have, but it could be one of the following:

- ✓ The person thinks that it was so weird for me to lay my hands on them that they just told me they got better rather than let me do a repeat heal.
- ✓ That my body has so much electricity in it from being struck by lightning and being electrocuted on a number of occasions (other stories not in this book!) that this surplus electricity helps the healing process, like the magnets some people use.
- ✓ That my guardian angel has some power to help people through me.
- ✓ Or more than likely they were going to get better anyway.

Saffy's breathing seemed to get better after I held her for about an hour. I sat down tired and sleepy and dozed. I was suddenly woken up by Saffy moving. She walked forward slightly and suddenly she knelt down. My first thought was to get her up as the vet had told me not to let her lay down. However, something told me to let her do it and she got down and lay on her bedding. I watched her for another half an hour and she suddenly started to roll over. I moved out of the stable as I did not want to get inadvertently kicked by her as she rolled. Was this her final death throws?

Saffy gave an almighty push and rolled over on her back with her legs in the air and looked over to me. Was this to say goodbye? Not a bit of it, what did she do? She gave out an enormous fart, which went on for some time as all the gas in her guts vented out into the stable. Once it had finished she got up with a rush and came over to the door, nudging me and asking for her tea! I got a hay net and filled it with best hay and tied it up in the corner of the stable and she attacked it with a vengeance. I phoned the vet and told him what had happened and he came to give her an examination. He told me that in all his time as a vet he had never seen such a miracle. Saffy went out in the field the next morning as if nothing had happened.

Chapter 80
Three Wheels on my Wagon

A lot of trailers have four wheels and it is possible for them to travel along the road with only three wheels. One day I was bringing our pony Mandy and her foal Gina back from the Essex Show in our trailer when a wheel went past the car overtaking me. I turned to Gill and said, "Hey, look at that wheel, it looks just like the ones on out trailer." Sure enough it was one of ours as it had decided to come off and go faster that we were going.

A few years ago I was travelling along the A14 dual carriageway between Cambridge and Huntingdon following behind a car and flatbed trailer at about 70 mph. As the car and trailer was about to pass an articulated lorry, one of the trailer wheels came slowly away from the nearside and was going at the same speed as it slowly drifted behind the lorry. I slowed down as the lorry and car and trailer kept the same speed and pulled away from me. I watched, fascinated as the wheel continued to creep towards the verge still going at a high speed. Just as I expected it to hit the verge and thinking that it would then ricochet back into the road, a layby appeared and it continued to travel into the slip road.

Parked in the layby was a white box van and the driver looked as though he was having his lunch reading a paper. Suddenly, the wayward wheel hit a small object and bounced and as it got to about four foot in the air it hit the back of the box van. It was a rather exceptional explosion as the fibre glass back of the van burst into hundreds of fragments. The wheel continued on its path and flew over a thick hedge. The driver must have jumped out his skin!

Sitting there minding his own business!

It must have taken me about 5 miles to catch up the car and trailer and then make hand signals to him, which he thought was me being rude at first, until he realised what I was trying to say. I then continued on my way up north. As I drove on, my thoughts turned to that poor van driver and imagined what happened next.

Driver: "Boss, I was parked in a layby having my snap (lunch) when suddenly the back of my box van exploded. It was such a shock and I assumed that someone had crashed into the back of me. When I got out expecting to see another vehicle, no one was there and I could not find any reason why it happened."

Boss: "I've heard of some fanciful stories from my drivers when they smash up my vans but this beats the lot, now what really happened?"

Chapter 81
The Danish Barge

My profession as an earthmoving geek has taken me into many different situations which one would not normally associate with someone who just digs holes in the ground. I have had to climb up precarious structures, go underground into unlit chambers and sewers. I have attended a banquet in a railway tunnel under Stansted Airport, sweated in 45-degree heat breaking rocks in the Dubai desert and got involved with the Belfast protection racketeers. This next story may interest you.

We had to replenish a beach in Norfolk. The beach sand was going to be dredged from the North Sea and shipped into a channel in The Wash. However, to get the sand from the dredger to the beach required some large flat-bottomed barges called a flat top dumb barge to transport it onto the beach. These barges are hard to come by and are about 100 metres long, 15 metres wide and sit out of the water about three metres unloaded. We searched for some and eventually I got a call from Alan who was arranging the dredging and he told me that he had found some in Denmark. He suggested that we fly over and look at them, so we booked in with a budget airline from Stansted and flew to Copenhagen.

We arrived in Copenhagen and were picked up by the shipping agent for the barges. He suggested that as one of them was moored up the coast we should look at that one first. As we did not know what to expect and was returning the same day we did not have any special clothing as it was sunny in Essex when we left. After about an hour's drive we arrived at this little jetty sticking out into a now rain swept Baltic Sea. The barge was anchored about quarter of a mile out into a heaving sea. We got out of the car and looked at a small motor boat coming towards us, disappearing behind the waves and then reappearing on the top of them. I thought, *What is that idiot doing in this sea in that bath tub, they must be mad.*

Our agent then said, "Right you guys, as the boat comes towards the jetty, get ready to jump aboard onto the bow and then into the cockpit!" What! I looked at Alan and he looked at me.

"He is joking right?" said Alan. So as the little boat's bow touched the jetty we jumped in turn into the cockpit. Up and down we went towards the barge, shivering in the rain soaked wind. I noticed that the only one wearing a lifejacket was the driver of the bathtub. We arrived at this monster of a barge with us heaving up and down. A farm tractor wheel was hanging down on a chain at the bows.

**A monster flat topped dumb barge –
Who are you calling dumb?**

The agent shouted over the noise of the sea and wind, "You've got to grab the tractor tyre and haul yourself up onto the barge. Wait for the boat to rise up on a wave and then grab!" I thought, *Oh God, if I miss the hold, I'm in the water without a lifejacket – better not miss then!* As the little boat rose up I grabbed the tyre and hauled myself up, slipping and sliding, onto the deck. Alan and the agent followed with me hauling them up.

Having walked about the barge from end to end and satisfied ourselves that it was suitable for what we wanted, the thought then struck me that we would have to repeat the process in reverse, climbing down that slippery tyre and jumping into the little boat. I don't know which was worse jumping up onto the tyre or down from it into a titchy boat that would not keep still. Ah well I survived it all, but at the time it was a little bit scary.

211

One hundred metres of heaving steel

Just to complete the story, we then headed back to Copenhagen as the next barge was moored in a dock in the middle of the city. We had to go through a large construction site to get to the barge and Alan and I told the agent that we had not brought any PPE (Personal Protective Equipment) with us like hard hat and boots. The agent said, "We don't do all the stupid health and safety stuff over here like you do in Britain, let's see what the manager thinks." So we went into the site office and saw the construction manager. He told us that he was quite happy for us to go through his site to look at the barge but he would need to give us a health and safety lecture before we could go onto his site and it went like this. *"There could be hazards on his site so don't trip over anything and also there is just a scaffold board gang plank onto the barge so don't fall in the water, thank you and off you go."* Did we need PPE, we asked. *"No, you need common sense,"* he said.

Oh, if we could have that attitude in this country, life would be easier. However, I must admit that the incident with the first barge could have had a bit more Health & Safety attached!

Chapter 82
The Shooting Stick

Cecil was a local gamekeeper and I am sure he will not mind me saying that he was a bit cantankerous sometimes, but he was a dear old boy and he told me lots of interesting country tales. Giles was a Master of Foxhounds and could be a bit snobbish and superior sometimes, but again he was a very interesting man and a fine horseman.

Before the hunting ban came into force, the relationship between a Master of Foxhounds (MFH) and a gamekeeper was always a delicate affair because the MFH wanted foxes to hunt and the gamekeeper wanted to exterminate all the foxes because they killed his game birds. A balance had to be struck to satisfy both field sports and many heated discussions ensued.

Cecil did not like the hunt and did not want any foxes on his patch, but his boss wanted to impress both the hunt and his pheasant shooters, so Cecil had to leave some of the foxes for the hunt. He had lots of very heated exchanges with Giles and he often told me that he hated him. Sadly Cecil passed away in his 80s and he willed a few of his possessions away to his friends. One of these was a good quality and sturdy shooting stick and he left it to my friend Connie. She often used it when we went point-to-point racing, sitting on it when we stopped to have a drink and a bite to eat.

One sunny day we all went to a point-to-point meeting and our little group of race goers were drinking, eating and chatting away, when Giles walked by. "Giles!" Connie shouted, "Come and have a drink with us." So he came over and asked for a whisky and a sausage roll. He commented that his legs were giving him a bit of trouble so Connie told him to sit on her shooting stick and take the weight off his feet so he accepted.

Giles was in good spirits and was leaning back on the stick telling one of his stories with great gusto when suddenly there

213

was a loud *CRACK!* as the shaft of the stick snapped. Giles's glass and sausage roll went upwards as he went downwards flat on his back. Everybody started to laugh and then quickly stemmed it because Giles was clearly in some pain, after all he was well over 70 years old. We picked him up and he wobbled back to his car mumbling something about how stupid it was to have a rotten shooting stick. Luckily, the remaining shaft of the stick did not do more damage by entering his nether regions??!!\

Woodworm doesn't work that quickly – does it?

Now think about this. Do you believe in the afterlife or ghosts or spirits? Well I must say that my guardian angel seems real to me and if Cecil wanted to get his own back on someone, Giles was the one he would have gone for. That stick was perfectly OK until that fateful day when it suddenly had a bad dose of woodworm!

Chapter 83
Early Flying Attempts – or Not

I seemed to have wanted to fly almost from birth and my father encouraged me by making small models of balsa gliders that I attempted to fly. This led to me building larger models and then learning to glide in my late teens.

Balsa model gliders being test-flown

The perceived dangers of flying did not dampen my enthusiasm for it and when I travelled to Majorca with my family in 1966 for a holiday, we had a little incident that would test some people's confidence. We were about to take off from Palma airport on the way home and the aircraft started down the runway. As we reached about halfway I turned to my mother and said, "This plane's not going fast enough to take off," and she asked me how I knew. I just said that I just knew. Suddenly the aircraft started to brake and swerved at the end of the runway onto the taxiway. It slowly taxied back with fire engines following us either side. Apparently the brakes had stuck on and the fire tenders had to hose them down to cool them off.

In 1969 I was camping at the National Model Aeroplane Championships on RAF Hullavington Airfield in Wiltshire when one of my mates came over and said he had heard that there was a WW2 Avro Lancaster bomber in one of the hangers. We waited until dusk and walked over to the hanger and found a side door open. We crept inside and there in the middle of the enormous space it the glare of our torches was a white Lancaster. We then found our way into the fuselage and up to the pilot's seat, banging our heads on just about every piece of aluminium framework. It was a surreal experience and we came out of that hanger very different than when we went in. That aircraft is now at East Kirkby museum in Yorkshire and they are hoping very soon to restore it to flying condition.

My love of flying was curtailed during the many years of horse riding but it remained with me. I remember competing in a dressage competition one sunny day when an aircraft flew over. On my score sheet was a comment from the judge, it read, 'The rider should not look upwards when carrying out a dressage test.'

Dressage points deducted for looking at aeroplanes during the test

Chapter 84
Flight Training Adventures

It was all Gill's fault; she was the culprit who got me back into flying. After I sold Saffy I started to get a bit bored and for my birthday she bought me a flight in a Tiger Moth (you know, the type of aeroplane that crashed at Challock Lees Chapter 22) and just to reinforce it she then bought me another Tiger Moth flight and then a flight in a Zlin which is a Czechoslovakian aerobatic aircraft. The pilot asked me what aerobatics I wanted to do and I said, "Everything," so he did. Then if that was not enough, she bought me a flying lesson – I was hooked.

Having discussed my course of lessons with other pilots since I gained my licence, we all seemed to make similar mistakes during our training. However, I had to have a few things unique to me, didn't I? My instructor was a great guy called Brian who is a rather ancient commercial pilot (sorry Brian), who incidentally, helped to fly a WW2 B17 Flying Fortress across the Atlantic back to the states. He suffered my ineptitude for 18 months until I qualified, so he is a very patient man.

One day he decided that we would take a cross-country navigation flight from our Andrewsfield base to Old Buckenham airfield in Norfolk. We took off and I managed to navigate my way to the vicinity of the airfield when I called up the tower. They asked me to wait by circling the Tacolneston TV/Radio mast north of the airfield because parachutists were just about to make a jump from 13,000 feet. They told me they would let me know when I could approach the airfield. I found the mast which is about 600 foot high and circled it at 1000 feet.

A few minutes later we heard the jump aircraft's radio say that they were about to discharge their load – no they weren't – yes they were – no, going around again…and so it went on. Round and round the mast we went being patient. Apparently, the cloud was starting to build up and the jump plane could not see the airfield to release their parachutists. At the same time the cloud was getting lower and to keep clear of the mast I gradually reduced my height keeping a good lookout to avoid colliding with it. After what seemed to be an age, the parachutists jumped and we still circled the mast. After another 5 minutes, Brian called up the tower and asked if we could come in. Oh! They said we had forgotten about you, yes of course come straight in.

When I was paying my landing fee, I mentioned that we were circling the TV mast for the past 10 minutes at mast height due to the low cloud and the two guys looked at each other and said, "Oh blimey, the International Rugby is on at the moment and you have probably blocked out the transmission for most of Norfolk, there's going to be hell to pay."

You've stopped them watching the rugby!

I slunk off to the café to find Brian talking to a chap from our airfield who had come in his tiny aerobatic biplane. He was just finishing a hearty late breakfast while we had a cup of tea. "See you back at Andrewsfield," we said as we both departed the clubhouse.

The fast little biplane took off in front of us and we made our way back via Ipswich and Colchester in our slow Cessna 152. On the way back our radio decided it would play up and we could only get every other word from air traffic control. As we tuned onto our airfield's frequency, we heard 'Golf Alpha – hisssss – go to – hisss – outhend' then 'Gol – hisss – Charlie you go – hisss

– plford,' 'Negative – hissss – Earls Colne is full up go to – hisssss,' 'That's funny Brian, what's up?' so we listened some more. 'It sounds as though they have a problem at Andrewsfield.'

So Brian called them up, "Golf Sierra Hotel Alpha Romeo, inbound from Old Buckenham, request airfield information." and what we got back was something like 'Golf – hissssssssss – Can't come here – hisssss – go to – hisss – end.' Brian turned to me and said, "Looks like something has happened back at base."

We eventually landed in the darkening light at a small farm airfield at Rayne and were taken by car back to Andrewsfield a few miles away. Sure enough as we drove down the road to the clubhouse, under floodlights was the little aerobatic biplane which had crashed on the runway. I wondered if the pilot had kept hold of his late breakfast.

Chapter 85
Overloaded in a Cessna 172

Just after I qualified for my pilots licence I was able to take passengers up with me. That means that in a four-seat Cessna 172 I could take three victims plus me up in the air to show off my neat flying skills. Proud of my qualification, I boasted about it to friends and family looking for Guinea pigs to take up. Amazingly there were a number of fools letting me hold their lives in my hands. Most of these early flights were uneventful but then pride comes before a fall and the next story is the first time I have ever told it and I apologise now to all the people who very nearly gave their lives in the cause of my stupidity.

I originally intended to take two passengers in a hired Cessna 172 one Sunday, Roy and Nigel, but Nigel told me that he had told another chap about the flight whom I knew from some years back and asked if he could come as well. Thinking back to when I knew Richard years ago, he was a lithe skinny chap although on the tall side. I estimated the weight of each victim and calculated how much fuel I could take on without being overloaded before the great day.

I got the plane ready before they all turned up and fuelled it up to my calculations for weight and went into the clubhouse to wait for them. One of the instructors came over to me and mentioned that the runway was very wet and boggy after all the recent rain. Roy, Nigel and Richard turned up all excited and chatting and I noticed that Richard had obviously been eating lots of pies since the last time I saw him. Now at this point I should have re-assessed the situation and what have we got – an overloaded aircraft and a boggy runway. I could not remove some of the fuel and now they were asking me if they could take other weight items such as their cameras etc. The take-off was going to be long and difficult.

I understand that the other pilots in the clubhouse were having bets on whether I would make it or not. They watched me slowly increase speed down the runway and halfway down we went past the clubhouse still on the ground. Apparently the audience were making comments such as, "Is he going to realise he won't make it and stop?" and, "Bet he ends up in a heap, wedged in the earth bank at the end of the runway!"

Three quarters the way down the runway, I was having serious doubts that I would take off when the hand of my guardian angel unsucked the aeroplane from the bog and we were airborne – phew! She climbed slowly upwards with comments from my passengers such as, "Cor! It feels great to be flying." Little did they know how close to death they had been. We climbed out and headed north towards Cambridge. It was a clear day and I had got all my radio frequencies and route written down on my kneeboard. We flew past Stansted, Haverhill, Cambridge and onto Ely. Things were going well and all my victims were having fun. Past Ely I turned west towards Chatteris. There is a parachuting site there and I knew I had to turn south long before I got there. I was talking to Cambridge radar and the controller reminded me to avoid Chatteris.

Suddenly, one of my victims said, "Oh look Mike there's a parachutist – and another one."

"Where, where?" I shouted and looked out of the front window above me. Sure enough, the sky was full of people dangling on bits of multi coloured cloth and string. Ahhhhhhh! I looked out to my left, found that I was not going to chop up a body and screamed the aircraft into a tight left turn away from them. Lots of words came into my head telling me what an idiot I was. This was not my best day. The journey back was a bit quiet with everyone thinking what might have been.

OMG! Parachutists!

Fair play to them all, it was not until a few years later that they all told me that they thought they were going to die during that take off run, so they kept that quiet as well. I learnt an awful lot that day.

Chapter 86

Aerobatics

When I had a flight in the Zlin, the expert pilot went through a fantastic aerobatic routine. We did loops, spins, rolls, handbrake turns well everything in the book. I loved it, as I thought I was in safe hands. During my flying training, I learnt mild manoeuvres such as stalls and spins just so I could get myself out of trouble if I did something stupid...who me??

After I'd had my pilot's licence for about a year I thought I would learn how to do aerobatics myself. My instructor was Gerald, he is Dutch, an airline pilot, a flying instructor, a real ale beer drinker and an all-round good egg, except that he is slightly bonkers – well he must have been to take me on.

I was being taught on a Cessna 150 Aerobat aircraft and Gerald's teaching was going quite well with loops, spins, stall turns and other aerobatics but then it came to the roll. I built up speed in a dive, levelled off, pushed the stick over and we started to roll. Once upside down and to stop the nose going down I had to give it down elevator and then relax it when coming round the right way up. Could I get it right and give it down elevator – could I heck. Every time I managed to give it up elevator and we went into an inverted dive. Gerald told me that nothing made him airsick...except my rolls. After about six lessons, we agreed that if we both wanted to survive we should give up with my aerobatic training.

He still talks to me though but has that 'You're an idiot' expression on his face.

Chapter 87
Jumping Without a Parachute

I had gained my pilot's licence in 2004 and the problem with hiring an aircraft is that you need to book it up on a certain day at a certain time, usually at the weekend when everyone else wants them. As is my luck, most of the time the weather was poor just during the hour that I had booked it. I was getting frustrated that I could not use my nice new licence to take victims, I mean passengers, up in the air. I was also not getting many flying hours in.

In 2005 I had done a few lucrative jobs and I had a bit of money saved up so I decided to buy my own aircraft. My wife Gill thought this was a very good idea and started checking the details of my life insurance policy. After looking at a few aircraft in this country I found out that the good ones were expensive and the ones I could afford were not in great condition. I then started to look on the internet and late one evening I found a cheap one in Chicago USA. It appeared to be in great condition from the photos. I showed it to Gill and she told me to, "Go for it." Obviously, she had found that the life policy had a good pay out.

What a lovely airplane!

I arranged with the aircraft sales company to fly into O'Hare Airport Chicago and they would meet me there and take me to see the plane. A few days before I was to leave, a client phoned to say he needed urgent help with a contract and as my clients paid me and the aircraft was a frivolous item, I emailed the sales company to tell them I would have to change my flight. I did not receive a reply and I assumed they thought I was a time waster.

Two weeks later they contacted me explaining that they had all been asked to help out as helicopter pilots during the Hurricane Katrina disaster and that's why they did not reply to my emails. So after an inspection by an independent surveyor, I purchased the aircraft without seeing it! The purchase of this aircraft was a long and difficult process for someone who had no knowledge of shipping it in a container and re-building the plane. I could have had it flown across the Atlantic via Newfoundland, Greenland, Iceland and Scotland but I did not want to be responsible for a ferry pilot being lost in a large ocean if the engine happened to fail.

Suffice to say that after it was put together over here, I wrote an article about it for an aviation magazine called Today's Pilot. The article was entitled 'How NOT to buy an aeroplane.' Nothing I do seems easy. After my article appeared in the magazine it went out of circulation. I hope it was not my fault!

The first time that I saw my purchase was when it arrived in its container at the aircraft maintenance hangers. I opened the doors in trepidation and we found a very nice aircraft albeit slightly damaged in transit. Eight months later I was flying my own plane.

It was not until after I had sent my money over to the states that I decided to find out if the aircraft had any accidents. The FAA website stated, 'Accidents: 1' – 'Damage to aircraft: Nil' – 'Fatalities: one.' How could an aircraft have an accident that killed someone and not have any damage?

After some investigation, I discovered that the aircraft was owned by a bail bondsman or bounty hunter. He had flown from Tulsa to Oklahoma in 1976 to arrest a young man who had jumped bail.

The bounty hunter arrested this guy to take him back to Tulsa. He had another passenger who was an attorney and he handcuffed the prisoner and put him in the back seat. The prisoner kept saying that he did not want to go back to jail but the two in the front of the aircraft ignored him. As the aircraft was on final approach towards the runway and at 1500 feet, the prisoner opened the door and jumped. He did not survive.

I was shocked to learn that my aircraft was involved in such a horrible accident and it unsettled me a bit. After some thought I realised that it was not the aircraft's fault and I duly forgave her.

The rebuilding of my aircraft took some time and it was touch and go whether it would actually get a Certificate of Airworthiness from the CAA. However, after eight months of work by the maintenance crew, she flew again and I have a lovely aeroplane.

My aircraft was originally built at Wichita Kansas in March 1965 and it took its first flight a few days before I left secondary school. We were both set free during that week.

Chapter 88
Lincolnshire from 250 Feet Up

One day I was asked to go to a business meeting in Lincoln and I decided that as the weather was forecast to be excellent, I decided to fly there. I phoned Mel who I was meeting and asked if he would pick me up from the local airfield at Wickenby. He said he would be delighted.

I took off from Andrewsfield the next day for the meeting in clear sunny weather after having checked the forecast in the morning, it was due to be like that all day. The flight was as smooth as silk and the visibility was excellent. I could see for miles. As I approached Spalding I could see all of the Wash, Norwich, Nottingham and the whole east coast. There was not a cloud in the sky. I was talking to the RAF radar guys at RAF Marham and then RAF Coningsby using the Barnsley area QNH. At this point I need to explain all about ALTIMETERS.

An altimeter is a dial positioned in front of the pilot with all the other instruments. It works like a barometer and is affected by the pressure of the air bearing down on a small metal disc filled with a vacuum. During low pressure weather systems the needle points to a low reading such as 950 millibars. During a high-pressure system it could read as high as 1030 millibars.

What a pilot needs to know is the height above either sea level or aerodrome ground level. Before the pilot takes off the altimeter has to be set to the current pressure which he gets from the aerodrome traffic control. This is set by a knurled knob on the instrument. If the aerodrome is 300 feet above sea level, then when the correct value is set, the pointer of the altimeter will read 300 feet. This setting is called the QNH. However, before a pilot lands at an aerodrome, he will re-set the knob to the pressure of the airfield so that he knows the height above the ground and not above sea level. He again gets this from the airfield traffic control. This is called the QFE. Just to confuse matters more, the military use an AREA QNH which is different from the other two and is the maximum pressure. Now I have either confused you or bored you.

**An altimeter showing a height of 300 feet
on a pressure setting of 1009 millibars**

I was happily flying along with the Area Barnsley QNH set on the altimeter at about 4000 feet and noticed a few wispy clouds appearing from the west a few thousand feet below. As I flew further, the clouds started to thicken up but it did not concern me much because I was nearly at my destination. As I signed off from RAF Coningsby, I started to descend and changed my radio frequency to Wickenby. I called them up to get the aerodrome QFE so that I would know how high above the ground I was, but I did not get any answer. I checked the frequency and called again – no answer. As this was going on I had descended and the cloud suddenly thickened up and enveloped me. I was in thick cloud and I was not qualified to fly blind.

I was suddenly in a situation where I was in cloud, descending and had the altimeter set to the wrong height! I had to decide whether to climb out of the cloud or keep descending while still calling up Wickenby. I did not think that I would keep the aircraft level if I climbed, so I descended.

I suddenly burst out of the base of the cloud and had a shock! I was just above the trees and a bungalow went past at high speed. I estimated that I was at 250 feet. I grabbed the chart to see if there were any tall masts around and I was still calling Wickenby when I saw a runway to my left. *Right,* I thought, *I'm going to land on that whatever happens.* Missing the trees, I positioned for the runway and as I came over the threshold I noticed it had a large 16 on it. If it was Wickenby, I should have been on runway 21!

Blimey! I'm at bungalow height

As I landed with a great sigh of relief the controller came over the radio and said, "Welcome to Wickenby, I hope I was not missed as I was otherwise engaged! Please taxi to the stands." My altimeter read 300 feet above the ground. I then noticed I was sweating a bit. I taxied in and parked. As I got out, Mel walked up to me a said,

"Hi Mike, you certainly picked fantastic weather." I looked up and saw there was not a cloud to be seen in the clear blue sky...

Chapter 89
Into a Thunderstorm

I had another meeting in Widnes near Liverpool and again I decided to fly there. I had been to Liverpool John Lennon Airport a number of times with no issues. During this trip I was flying between canyons of fluffy cumulus cloud. I was at 4000 feet with the cloud either side of me going up thousands of feet above me.

With about 15 miles to go, I called up Liverpool Approach to let them know I was inbound. They gave me the airfield information and I started to descend. I looked ahead and saw bright clear blue sky but there was a dark band of cloud below this but it only looked about 100 foot thick. I had to decide whether to fly over or under it. If I flew over it, I would have to descend very quickly to get into Liverpool, so I decided to descend and fly under it. I slowly descended and I got to 1500 feet just as I arrived at the dark clouds.

Expecting to see clear blue sky under it, what I found was pure hell and the whole cabin instantly became pitch black. Rain was thrashing against the aircraft and lightning was all around me. I was staring at the horizontal attitude instrument keeping the aircraft level when I just about heard Liverpool calling me up over the noise of the rain. There was no way I was going to lose concentration by answering the radio, so I left it. The storm went on and on and then suddenly I saw a tiny glint of light ahead and over to the left. I headed straight for it and eventually I burst out into brilliant sunlight and crystal clear blue sky.

The light at the end of a tunnel!

I gave a sigh of relief and called up Liverpool Approach apologising for my delayed reply. They wanted to let me know about a serious storm cell that had gone through their airspace heading towards me. I thanked them for their concern and told them that I had just gone through it! Cessna aircraft are tough thank God.

Chapter 90
Lunch on the Isle of Wight

One of the great delights about flying is that you can take off and go to some distant location for lunch. Many of my mates pop over to Le Touquet for some seafood and French cuisine, but I tend to stay in this country. One weekend at Easter my 80-odd-year-old mother was staying with us and we woke up on the Saturday and the weather was beautiful. I asked her if she wanted to go for lunch on the Isle of Wight and she said, "That will be nice dear."

We took off in glorious weather and had a very calm flight with little turbulence and unlimited visibility. We landed at the little grass airfield behind Sandown and ordered a taxi into town. When we arrived it was obvious that because of the weather, the beaches were busy and so were the restaurants. Rather than queue, we walked slowly along the beach to bide our time in the hot sunshine. Eventually, we arrived back at the line of sea view restaurants along the promenade and picked one that seemed to by now, have a table available. We sat under a parasol and ate a wonderful lunch looking out to sea.

When we finished, I went to pay but my mother insisted that she should pay. As it is no point arguing with my mother, I let her go into the restaurant while I waited for her outside. There were some steep steps leading down from the patio area onto the pavement, so I thought I would wait at the top and make sure mother did not fall down them. I was just thinking how steep they were when there was a scream from behind and I turned around to see mother laying on the ground. A crowd of diners immediately started to surround her as I ran back to her. As soon as I saw that her foot was not pointing in the right direction, I knew she had badly broken her ankle. Instead of falling down the steep steps, she had misjudged a step at the doorway which was only a few inches high. We made her a bit more comfortable and called an ambulance. Waiting for it I phoned my wife Gill. "Hi Gill, we have a little problem. Mum has tripped over and broken her ankle so I may be home a bit late."

The ambulance took her and me to Newport hospital and she was seen quickly by the doctors. "Your mother will need to have an emergency operation and she will be here for some time," the doctor told me. Oh! Rollocks, the only way to and from the island is either by ferry or plane. It then dawned on me that visiting her would be interesting. After she told me what she needed for a stay in hospital, I left her as she went into the operating theatre. By now it was 4 o'clock and I phoned for a taxi to get me back to the airfield. I arrived back at Andrewsfield at 6 o'clock, collected Gill from home and travelled the 35 miles to my mother's home to collect her things.

The next few weeks was spent by me flying over to Sandown every few days and getting a taxi to Newport to visit her. The first time I flew in and got into the taxi, the driver said, "You're the guy whose mother broke her ankle in Sandown and she is in Newport hospital." At that point I realised that I was on an island with the island jungle drums going full tilt.

Chapter 91
Giving George Some Flying Advice

My wife Gill has a cousin who has a daughter who was planning to marry George. He is a very quiet, gentlemanly young man from Nigeria who decided that he wanted to become an airline pilot. He took himself off to the USA to gain his private pilot's licence and then came back to this country to get some hours in before going on to get his commercial licence. One day at a family get together, I offered to fly with him so he could build up some confidence for flying in British weather as opposed to the beautiful sunny Florida weather that he learnt in.

Our first excitement happened when he flew me to Shoreham airport on the south coast in my Cessna. The runway we were using was to the north so our final approach was over the sea, which can give a pilot a very strange vertigo feeling. There was also a severe crosswind coming from the east and George was pilot in command and sitting in the right hand seat. Halfway down the final approach he suddenly told me that he could not continue as the crosswind was so strong and blustery and he handed control over to me.

To be suddenly given control of an aircraft on final approach, sitting in the 'wrong' seat was a bit of a shock. I had to reverse all my actions such as my left hand on the throttle and my right hand on the control yoke which I was unused to. I was struggling with the crosswind when another vibration started. Was it the engine? No, it was my knees knocking together! They were completely out of my control and they stayed rattling until we were down on the runway.

George then bought a share in a Piper PA28, a low wing aeroplane located at Blackbushe airfield west of London. One day I flew over there to fly with him in his aeroplane. As soon as he did his checks I realised that he was not totally confident with the whole affair, but I let him carry on with the intention that I would take over if anything went wrong. His flying ability was very good but I had doubts about his 'situational awareness.' This means that he may not have been aware of what was going on outside and around him. I kept a beady eye on the surroundings instead and let him do the flying as I knew what an idiot I had been during my early flying attempts even after I gained my pilot's licence.

We were approaching the airfield on our return from our flight and I was aware that there were other aircraft in the circuit. Just as George was about to turn onto final approach another aircraft appeared on our right also on final approach. I pushed the throttle to full power and shouted, "I have control!" and pulled the aircraft up into a steep climb missing the other one by what felt like a few feet but was probably a lot more. We quietly did another circuit while the tower talked to George and asked him to come and see them after he had landed. He got a severe rollicking and learnt a good lesson.

George flew with me in my aircraft on many occasions and all the time my intention was to make him an all-round good pilot. One of his regular moans was that I always wanted to fly into short and difficult runways and he used to say, "Mike, why do I need to do this? I want to fly airliners and they have long runways."

He eventually gained his commercial licence and he got a job as first officer with a Nigerian airline flying internal flights in Africa. He told me that all the short runway landings he did with me enabled him to fly into the rough and tiny ones in Africa. The family is proud that he is now a very competent captain and has a great job with an airline in Dubai.

Chapter 92
Anything to Declare?

One Sunday our flying club decided to have a fly out to Lelystad north of Amsterdam in Holland. Shane and Rob, two mates of mine would come with me and we were all excited while we were donning our life jackets before entering the plane. However, after that things did not go so well.

The first incident was when Rob, who was used to a low wing aircraft walked straight into the trailing edge of the wing on my Cessna and sliced the top of his head. I had never used my aircraft's first aid kit before so this was a good chance to hone up on my surgery skills! I stemmed the blood and covered the flap of skin on top of his balding head with a number of sticky plasters. It looked a bit like a beige cowpat on top of his head but he could not see it, so it was OK.

The flight was not too bad as we dodged a few storms over France but halfway across Belgium I had an urge to have a pee. Keeping quiet, I calculated that with our headwind we would take another 45 minutes to arrive at Lelystad and my bladder was not going to make it. Excusing myself to the others I pulled out a plastic sick bag and pee'ed into it...and pee'ed, and pee'ed until the 12-inch-long bag was full. Now relieved, I tied the top of the bag into a knot and laid it gently on the floor.

When we arrived, we had to get some fuel, so we taxied over to the pumps to fill up. What struck me was the pristine condition of the concrete pavements, the pumps, the ladders and all the equipment needed for an airfield to operate. I looked across at the arrivals building and again this was pristine. They obviously take great pride in their airfield. While we were filling the tanks, one of the pilots from the other club aircraft came over and said, "You had better have all your paperwork in order, the Customs chap is being a stickler for correctness."

After filling up, we walked over to the arrivals building and into the customs area. The officer was immaculate in a smart mid blue uniform and he stood there waiting for us to check our paperwork and asked if we had anything to declare. Besides the paperwork, all I had was a foot long plastic sausage full of urine.

"Anything to declare?" – "Just a bag of urine."

I don't think I have seen such a look of disgust from anyone. He had obviously had to deal with the rest of our motely club members and this was the last straw. It was as if he was thinking, *These English, they are disgusting,* as he waved us on with contempt.

While Shane and Rob made their way to the restaurant, I went to the loos to empty my sausage. I thought about putting it into a waste bin but then saw that they too were pristine. I went into the sweet smelling gents and into a cubical so that I could empty my sausage in peace. I undid the knot and carefully turned it upside down into the loo pan. Nothing happened? I looked and realised that it was a self-sealing bag and I could not open it.

What to do? So I held the sausage between my legs and pointed the top down the pan. With my two thumbs, I pushed them into the plastic which turned out to be quite strong. Suddenly, my thumbs pierced the bag and a torrent of urine sprayed out all over the pan, the cistern, the walls, the floor and me! FFFFFFFFFFFF! I used a whole toilet roll in an attempt to clear it up without too much success. I suppose the loo cleaner later thought, *Those English, they are disgusting.*

Halfway back and flying over France, Rob went quiet and suddenly said, "Mike, have you got another sick bag?"

"Yes loads do you need one?" and as I turned around I could see that he needed one and quickly. The poor chap was suffering with concussion – and they say you should not fly with concussion.

Chapter 93
The Broken Spring

At weekends I often fly with my buddy Shane and we take it in turns to fly to somewhere and back. They call this type of flying 'The £100 pound bacon butty' because pilots go to another airfield, have one and then fly back. The cost is the fuel and the landing fee, therefore £100 just to eat a butty.

Recently, we decided to do just that and checked the aircraft out thoroughly with the checklist. I taxied to the runway hold and again checked everything including that my seat was secured. The previous week, an aircraft similar to mine had crashed on take-off and I speculated (wrongly as it turned out) that his seat had shot backwards and he had pulled the plane into a stall.

With this fresh in my mind, I again rattled the seat to make sure it was locked. I entered the runway and pushed in the throttle to full power. We raced down the runway and lifted off at 55 mph. The climb out is steep and at about 50 foot off the ground my seat suddenly shot backwards. Being small, my arm went to full length and I pulled the yoke backwards. This caused the aircraft to pitch up violently. We were about to stall.

Shane shouted, "NOSE DOWN!" and I shouted, "TAKE CONTROL!"

He pushed the yoke forward as fast as he could and the dear old thing wallowed about and picked up speed. We climbed away from near disaster. "Pwew!" said Shane, "What happened?" I was still trying to get my seat forward and told him what had happened. I felt down and found the spring holding the locking pin had broken and was just hanging there.

Shane had positioned the aircraft onto the downwind leg to land and I asked him if he was OK to land it from the right hand seat and he said, "Possibly." So I told him to set the aircraft up to land and I would take over just before we touched down. He followed me through on the controls just in case my seat moved and we landed just fine.

When we took the spring out I bent it to see how bad it was and it just snapped in two. The thing was obviously worn out after 50 years use. This little thing about two inch long is all that stops a seat moving backwards at the wrong moment.

Two new springs were obtained from the States and fitted to my seats and I have also had an inertia belt fitted which stops the seat running back if they do fail.

Shane is really glad I have a Guardian Angel looking over me and I am really glad I had Shane with me that day.

And yes, to all those pilots reading this, I did report the incident to the CAA.

Chapter 94
The Good Flying Days

I don't want you to get the impression that my flying is all bad and that I am totally hopeless. Far from it, as I now have over 800 hours of flight time logged. Most of these hours have been spent in sheer aviation bliss. Every time I fly, the weather and light conditions are different and this gives an ever-changing experience. As an example I will relate to you one of my best days.

In 2008 a work colleague and friend, Alastair arranged a meeting for us with a large transport company at their head office in Carlisle. The office was not far from Carlisle airport which the company also owned. The meeting was about the job in Widnes (remember the Storm, Thunder & Lightning – chapter 89 above). We decided to fly so we could get there and back in a day rather than driving and staying overnight. The weather happened to be that one day every year when the sky is clear with little wind and unlimited visibility.

We flew at 4000 feet up the east coast past Peterborough, The Wash, Lincoln, York and onto Scotch Corner where we turned left over the Yorkshire Dales to Penrith. We were talking to Newcastle radar over the Dales and he told us about a fast moving jet fighter coming from our 6 o'clock. That's behind us! Hoping that the jet would see us, we held our breath until he passed underneath us 1000 feet below. We watched this jet playing and having fun zooming around the Dales.

In front of us were the Lake District Mountains, some with a little bit of snow still on the peaks. Behind us we could clearly see the east coast, the North Sea and Newcastle. The Dales and Pennines stretched north and south away from us with their bleak vegetation. We could easily see for 50 miles. On a day like this it is very good to be alive and to be able to witness the spectacle of nature from above.

At Penrith we turned north for Carlisle and in 15 minutes we were on the ground at the airport. We were picked up and driven to the office for the meeting. Our trip home was just as spectacular as we retraced our flight in the same weather as we came up in. We landed back at Andrewsfield without any tiredness or stress, which we would have had if we had driven all that way. It took us three hours to get there and two hours 20 minutes to get back. Assuming that there were no traffic hold ups, it would have taken us six hours just to get there by car.

Then one day I took a work colleague to Selby in Yorkshire for a meeting. He had not flown in a light aircraft before and he decided not to tell his wife he was going by air. The flight was fantastic and he loved it. We landed at a little airfield about two miles from the office where we were to have the meeting. A guy from the office picked us up in his car and drove us along the narrow country lane at such a speed that we were both terrified. We got out at the other end all shook up and looked at each other hoping that we would not have to go through that hell again. However, the same guy took us back at the same break neck speed. We were both glad to get back in the plane.

He told his wife about flying to the meeting afterwards and I understand she was not impressed with him. I told Gill about the car drive and she checked out my life policy again.

Chapter 95
Lunch in a Railway Tunnel

During my long career in earthmoving I have had so many interesting experiences that I could not dream of writing them all down. My job to an outsider would be considered as boring, just digging holes in the ground all day, but it is more than that and I have been involved in a number of notable projects.

Between 1986 and 1991 I was a project manager developing Stansted Airport from a minor airfield into the international airport it is today. I was involved in managing virtually all the earthworks which included the runway, taxiways, the terminal building, roads, sewers, lakes, car parks, hangers and many other constructions. One of them was the construction of the railway line which was tunnelled under the airport and the runway.

The airport authorities wanted to open the tunnel in style and someone thought that a re-creation of Isambard Kingdom Brunel's 1843 banquet held in the first tunnel ever constructed under a river running from Rotherhithe to Wapping under the Thames, would be a good idea.

So they did and I, along with other workers, were invited to see the tunnel boring machine cut the last section at the north portal, the first train to run from the main line up to the tunnel entrance and then we had the banquet inside the south part of the tunnel. It was memorable day.

1843 Brunel's Thames Tunnel banquet

1990 Stansted Railway Tunnel banquet

As an aside, to all you modern hi-tech people out there, I was given my first company mobile phone in 1986 which consisted of a small suitcase called a Motorola 4500X. I lugged the thing around the site for many years until one day I asked my assistant (who was my company owners nephew) to get it from my car. As he walked back across the car park, he swung it around his head and the handle came off and it crashed to the ground – after that I did not need to lug it around all day – RESULT!

Chapter 96
The Skyline Drive

Gill and I went to the USA in 1989 to see our friends in Indianapolis. After we stayed with them for a few weeks, we hired a car and travelled around the east coast area. I had been having a bit of trouble getting into the car and usually ended up sitting in the passenger seat. Having driven a million miles getting in the right hand side of a car, driving on the 'wrong' side was proving difficult. However, as all the other vehicles were driving on the wrong side of the road I was OK once I started driving because it was difficult for me to drive on the correct side as all the natives tended to get a bit upset and hooted at me.

We drove to Virginia to see another friend up in the Blue Ridge Mountains. The next day before we travelled up to New York we decided to go along the Blue Ridge Mountains Skyline Drive with the Shenandoah Valley to the west. This road has some of the best views in the USA and the winding road was constructed purely to take in these views. We were warned to look out for deer and bear and to drive carefully.

Off we went, driving along the winding roads, saying *ooo!* and *ahhh!* as we rounded the bends and seeing the magnificent views. We did not see many cars and trucks, but the ones we did see were going like the clappers. Obviously the locals have got used to the views.

We came round a bend and saw some deer crossing the road, so we decided to pull over and watch them. After a while we got back in the car and off we went again. After travelling along the winding road for about half an hour and looking sideways enjoying the scenery, Gill suddenly said, "What side of the road are we supposed to travelling on?!" Oh eff!! I'm on the wrong side!

I swerved over to the right side of the road and we both looked at each other as a few minutes later a truck came tearing round a bend. Had we not changed lanes, I don't know if we would have survived. "NEWS FLASH! BRITS DIE BECAUSE THEY WERE DRIVING ON THE WRONG SIDE OF THE ROAD!"

Chapter 97
Norway

Gill and I decided to treat ourselves and go on a cruise to see the Northern Lights in Norway. It was February 2012 so it was going to be a bit cold up in the Arctic. We sailed from Tilbury docks and over to Amsterdam for a day trip and then onto Norway. The trip was for two weeks and for 10 out of the 14 days poor Gill was seasick. We had a force 9 gale on the way there and a force 10 on the way back. The ship was heaving up, down and side to side constantly. There was nothing I could do except give her sympathy and warm thin soup. However, when we entered the fiords the sea became calm and she was able to get up, eat and go ashore. Of course, it would not have been normal for me to not have an accident or two, would it?

My first accident occurred in Tromso. Gill and I walked around the town in the snow and ended up in the shopping mall (now that is unusual for Gill who is a shopaholic??). We looked around the shops and made our way up onto the top floor where we found a café. After purchasing our drinks and sandwiches, we sat at a table on a balcony overlooking the rest of the mall. Having our outside coats on, we took them off and laid them on a chair together with our snow sticks.

As we got up to leave, I pulled at the coats and one of the snow sticks fell through the balustrade out into space. I watched in horror as the stick whirled around heading at high speed straight for a woman with two children sitting on a bench. There was a crash and a scream! I sent Gill down to find out how much body damage I had achieved and my mind was wondering what the Norwegian Police cells looked like.

My guardian angel had luckily come to Norway with me as it missed the children by a hairs breath. Gill apologised profusely to the shocked woman and told her that her husband was an accident waiting to happen. I sheepishly came down the escalator

247

and added my humble apologies, trying to look like the idiot that I was.

Our next stop was Alta in the North Cape and after another rough few days Gill was very unwell. One of the trips we had booked was to go on a self-drive husky sledging trip. As she could not go, the ships agent re-sold her place to another person. We boarded the coach and travelled through the snow to a remote farmstead. Everyone else was in pairs except me and this little old lady called Jane. She was small, about 80 years old but obviously very game. She had been on the cruise liner for months, travelling up the Amazon, around the Caribbean Islands and now in the Arctic.

They then split us up into two teams and I was in the second. As soon as I saw the huskies and the sledges I knew that an accident could happen. The dogs were so keen that they were all barking and straining at the sledge reins. I have a little video of the first group starting off and it shows dogs, people and sledges crashing into each other – what fun!

Part of our instruction was that one person would sit in the sledge while the other drove it. We were told that the driver must not get off the sledge as the dogs would run off out of control and the passenger would not be able to stop them as he/she would be just lying in the sledge. The only control the driver had was two brakes. One consisted of a rubber pad which by pushing down with a foot could slow down the sledge and the other was a jagged piece of steel which you pushed down to stop the sledge and hold it like a hand brake. All very simple to understand – what?

When the others came back from their run, it was our turn. The first shock was when Jane suggested that she should drive first and I could be the passenger. My heart sank as she did not seem to understand the simple instructions when they were being explained. There were six sledge combinations and we were at the back, last to go. As the instructor in the front put her arm up to go, Jane let off the brake and we overtook all the others, bumping into each one with me shouting *Bump!* "Sorry!" *Bump!* "Sorry!" *Bump!* "Sorry!" – "JANE, SLOW DOWN!"

The view from the sledge

I took a video of the sorry event. It shows my feet in front with four dogs out of control tearing down a snowy track with the instructor shouting at Jane to slow down. They had placed a photographer strategically at the top of a bank so he could get shots of the 'punters' coming towards him. Instead of taking photos the video shows him frantically waving his arm up and down to slow her up. There is then a scream and I am heading straight for a large tree, next second we crashed into it which stopped the dogs dead in their tracks.

Apparently, we had hit the top of the bank and Jane flew off sideways and damaged a tree with her head. She was dazed but we got her into the sedge and covered her up with Reindeer skins to keep her warm. We then carried on with the drive through wonderful snow covered fields and woods – with me driving this time! Next day I asked Jane how she felt and she said the ship's doctor told her to get a head x-ray when she got home as he thought she may have cracked her skull.

Still, it could have been worse – if I had not hit the tree and stopped the dogs, I may well have been carted off into the wilderness, never to be seen again! Bad luck – good luck!

Chapter 98
Two Bulls on Christmas Eve

One year Gill, her sister Beth and I decided rent a house in North Norfolk for Christmas just to get away from it all, do a bit of bird watching and a bit of rest and relaxation. That was the plan. The place we rented was the rear part of a grand Georgian mansion. The owners of the big house also came up from London for their Christmas. Next to our part of the house was a small grassed lawn and beyond that a wood and beyond that, a large paddock. We casually noticed that it had two very large bulls in it.

We came back from a day out shopping on Christmas Eve just as it was getting dark. We were looking forward to having a nice bit of steak for tea and then we had planned to go to the local church for Midnight Mass. As we approached the gates to our place, they were closed and the owners of the big house were waiting for us. The lady of the house and her aged mother explained that we could not go into our house as the two bulls had got out of the field and were in our garden and they had closed the gates on them. She suggested that we went into the big house to wait for either the farmer or the police. Gill and Beth duly followed her to her house but I thought that I may be able to get the bulls back into their field.

As I walked around the front of the big house to get into our garden, I met up with the owner's two sons who had just come up from London. I asked them if they would help me, which they said that they would but needed me to give them some advice on what to do as they were city boys and not country bred.

Nice Bull – come to Daddy

I got a walking stick out of my car and a couple of torches and the three of us went into the garden. The bulls had disappeared but we could hear them crashing through the wood, so we followed them. The wood had a lot of undergrowth in it and it was difficult walking in the pitch dark. We found them in the corner of the wood fenced in on three sides, so all we had to do was to keep them there until the farmer arrived.

After a short while I decided to leave the lads in charge while I found the hole in the fence so we could get them back in the field. I got a pair of bolt croppers and pliers out of my car (well everyone carries around those tools with them, don't they? Boy Scout motto 'Be Prepared!'). Eventually I found the hole in the fence and proceeded to cut it back to make it bigger. I then walked back to the bulls. I found the two lads walking back towards me. "Where's the bulls?" I said.

"They charged us and stampeded through the wood, we don't know where they have gone!" *Oh great!*

As we walked back to the big house the owner came out to inform me that she had been onto the police and they were sending out an armed response unit from Norwich. Apparently they always shoot loose bulls if they get on the public highway rather than let them cause a traffic accident. The two lads decided that they had had enough of looking after loose bulls so they decided to go into the house to enjoy their Christmas Eves party.

I couldn't let the police shoot them, so I decided to search for them, but how in the pitch dark?

I started to walk around the big house's sweeping drive and noticed that the gravel had been scuffed up. Then I saw some deep holes in the front lawn. As the ground was very wet, they were about a foot deep and about 6 inch wide just like postholes – yes the bulls had been right across the front lawn. I followed the holes down the edge of the main driveway and they ended at the entrance onto the road. Oh no! They must have got out onto the highway, which means they have a good chance of being shot! I went out into the dark road and looked each way. Hang on, if they had gone onto the road, there would be some mud splattered about but there was none?

I went back into the grounds and searched and found the postholes going into a large field. I followed them. After about half a mile I found them standing next to a hedge nice and quiet like. I walked to within 10 yards of them fully armed with a stick and a torch. We stood there for a while looking at each other. What next? If I could get them to turn around, I might just get them to walk back to the wood. I started banging my stick against my wellies and tried to get them to turn around. Suddenly, they started to move. Will they charge me? I looked around for an escape route and saw a big open field – Ah?

I kept smacking my wellie and they both slowly turned around and started walking straight back to the wood about a quarter of a mile away across the field. I followed some distance behind saying, "Good boys, keep walking towards the wood for Daddy." I made sure I walked to the left side of them as they were still making squelching sounding postholes in the wet soil with their feet. Then one of them must have deviated from a straight line as halfway across the field my leg went down one of the 'post holes'. As I fell I managed to twist around to prevent breaking my leg and I fell backwards into the mud. There I was flat on my back in the middle of a large field in the pitch black with no phone and no one knew where I was. Great! I thought of sending an SOS in Morse Code with my torch but who would see it? It turned out that Gill & Beth had no idea what I was up to – I had just disappeared when she went into the big house and the two boys didn't tell her I was out looking for bulls, but then nor did I!

After managing to extract myself, I walked back into the wood and there were the two bulls standing looking at the hole in their fence. I crept up behind them and went shoo! What did they do – startled, they bolted past the hole in the fence and back into the wood just where I first found them. Just then I saw lights coming across the bull's field – it was the farmer with his truck and a tractor. After explaining to him and his mate what had happened and that the police were on their way to shoot them, he told me that they were not dangerous and were two quiet calm boys who would not hurt a fly.

While his mate went over to the hole in the fence to make it bigger, the farmer asked me to shine his powerful lamp fixed to his truck onto the bulls in the wood while he got them. He said all he had to do was to rattle some feed in a bag and they would follow him back into the field, just like sheep. He walked into the wood and I shone the light on the bulls. He was calling them and rattling the bag of feed when the bulls suddenly charged him and he just managed to jump out of the way! Lots of swearing and shouting ensued.

Both men charged around the wood for the next half an hour while I shone the lamp on the bulls – when I could see them. In the end they had to take down a long line of fencing and eventually, the bulls were back into the field. The two men spent the whole of their Christmas Eve building fences. I walked back into our house and Gill said, "Where the heck have you been, we have been worried sick and we are waiting to cook dinner." I had a very late steak dinner and ate it completely exhausted with the occasional glare from Gill.

To round off that Christmas I decided to have an accident which should have seriously injured me, but again I was protected by my Guardian Angel yet again.

The wing of the hall we were staying in had very large rooms and high ceilings and in the centre of the sitting room was a metal framed glass coffee table about four foot by two foot.

The day before we were leaving we had packed everything away for an early start and it was late. I suddenly remembered that a book I had been reading was still on the bookshelf at the far side of the sitting room, so I went in and lazily did not put the lights on as I knew exactly where it was.

As I swept across the floor, my shin hit the glass table and I went crashing down on top of it, flat out. I think I must have damaged every part of my body on the metal corners but the glass, thankfully, did not break. As I lay on the floor, Gill came rushing in and turned on the lights. One look from her and she was gone saying, "What an idiot, serves you right, I can't believe you sometimes!" A little bit of sympathy, that's all I wanted but did I get it – No! Just – "Don't tell me I don't want to know, but you had better be able to drive us home in the morning."

Wimmin Huh!

Chapter 99
The Health & Safety Inspection

Health & Safety (H&S) – everyone I know complains about it. Whatever job you do or wherever you go, Health & Safety rules and regulations are in force. I worked in the civil engineering industry and it has grasped the H&S nettle with both hands and put it on a pedestal. A huge separate industry has grown up around it and I would estimate that 50% of the cost of any project is now used up on this strange phenomenon.

On the one hand it is difficult to criticise H&S as it is supposed to save people from injury and death. By criticising it we come across as not caring about the safety of workers and the general public. But on the other hand, in my opinion, it has gone too far, almost to a ridiculous extreme. Doesn't anyone have any common sense anymore?

H&S all started for me in 1985 whilst working on the St Neots Bypass. The main contractor's project manager called me into his office and told me that the company had issued an edict that everyone was to wear a hard hat from then on. We were working in open fields, nowhere near anything dangling overhead and I said, "What do you think will fall on my men's heads besides bird poo?" I held out for a week but in the end after being told that I would be banned from the site I had to give in. My men were not happy as the plastic helmets made their heads sweat and gave some of them headaches.

Since that date, more and more rules have come into force and now we have to wear full PPE (Personal Protective Equipment). On most construction sites the following PPE has to be worn at all times:

- ✓ Plastic hard hat, which must not be out of date
- ✓ Ear defenders if you are near any noise
- ✓ Impact glasses to protect the eyes

- ✓ Dust mask if there is any dust about
- ✓ Hi Viz coat with sleeves as no skin must be exposed to the sun
- ✓ Gloves to protect the hands from splinters and dirt
- ✓ Hi Viz full length trousers as shorts are not allowed
- ✓ Steel toe cap and sole boots

Working with all this gear on, sometimes becomes overwhelming for the workers. It may be 30 degrees in the shade but they have to keep it all on. Impact glasses makes uneven ground difficult to walk on as it distorts your vision and when it is raining, you just cannot see. Sweat build up on your hands often causes dermatitis and all the flashing beacons on the plant gives you headaches and sometimes causes epilepsy. I find the steel soled boots cause me to have painful feet and as we are not allowed to wear 'Rigger boots' the muddy water we have to work in fills up the boots and then the wet feet causes all sorts of foot rot.

But enough of my moaning! A few years ago I was working on a site in Southend excavating away some cliffs because they had slipped. The main contractor had a zero accident policy. They think that by stating this they will never have an accident. They can't be more wrong.

I was walking around the site with the main contractors H&S director and the subcontractor boss I was working for, carrying out an audit for health & safety. All was going well when halfway through I asked if I could be excused so that I could examine a part of the cliff that was being excavated to make sure it was stable. I walked over to the cliff face and stopped the excavator from working, studied the cliff and gave some instructions to the driver. As I turned around the high impact glasses I was wearing gave me a distorted ground line and I tripped over a lump of soil. Whack! I went down and I put out my right hand to soften the fall. I knew immediately that I had cracked a bone in my hand as I heard in go and felt the pain.

I quickly got up and the excavator driver asked if I was Ok. I told him I was. Looking quickly at my two colleagues I saw they were looking the other way and had not seen me fall over. Thank goodness! I stuck my throbbing hand into my pocket and re-joined them to complete the audit.

The next day I came into work with a tightly bandaged hand and the first thing that the project manager asked was, how did I hurt my hand and he hoped it was not on his site. I replied that I had fallen over at home and he was not to worry.

You may wonder why I lied. It was for a number of reasons, the main one being that the amount of forms I and others would have to fill in would take up a lot of time and I would have found this most boring. Secondly, the whole site would have been subject to an investigation which may have stopped all the work and I am sure that the main contractor would have banned all of the workers from walking on the site and that would have restricted progress further losing everyone time and money. I would also have been pestered by insurance companies hoping to make some money for them and for me. It would have all been too much to bother about for someone who has had a few accidents before. After all I was the one that tripped over so it must have been my fault or perhaps it was the stupid safety glasses!

Chapter 100
The Future?

So here we are, at the end of The Accident Book. I hope you have enjoyed it and you may have come to the conclusion that I might be accident prone. What does the future hold for me… "What's that, dear? Oh hang on a minute, can you, Gill is cooking spaghetti bolognese and has just asked me to grate some cheese…"

Sorry about that, but I'm back now. She asked me to grate some cheese for the spag bol and I asked her all the right questions such as, 'Where's the cheese, which one do I use, where the grater is and do I use the large holes or the small ones?' I was grating away when I sliced the top of my index finger. Blood everywhere, Gill shouting at me trying to stem the flow with the cheese, the grater and the worktop covered in blood, she trying to bandage it up when she realised that the spag bol was then burning so she had to open the kitchen door to let all the smoke out. Well I ask you, she claimed that it would have been much better to have done it herself. That's gratitude for you! I am now typing this last chapter with my middle finger as my index one has a large bandage on it.

Where was I? Ah yes, the future. Well I started this book by saying that I was born at the best possible time. Before that, there were a couple of wars and before that not very nice living conditions unless you were rich. Nowadays I look at the youngsters and see them playing all day on their iPads and phones because the world is now a dangerous place for little ones to just run wild. Will they have the adventures I and my contemporaries had?

I suppose they could if they really wanted to but their parents would probably stop them so they would have to wait until they were older. I think that's why some people do extreme sports to get an adrenaline rush, because they never experienced it when they were very young.

I consider my life to have been normal. All I have done is to have a steady job and done a few fairly conventional hobbies. I have never had to go to war, I have never been a member of the emergency services and I have never purposefully put myself into a dangerous situation to save someone. All those people are my heroes. My events have appeared suddenly from nowhere. OK I have been a bit of an idiot sometimes and with more thought, I may not have had a particular accident but I am still here at the moment, which is a bonus.

However, I don't think my guardian angel has quite finished with me yet and I may still have the big one yet to come. When it does, you may even read about it in the newspapers! In the meantime, stay safe and don't try to recreate any of these stories. As my disclaimer tells you at the front of this book I do not want to be taken to court by you after you have killed yourself!

And then there was the time when I made a Barn Owl nest box which turned out to be rather heavy. I had to get it up high into the barn, so I rigged up a pulley system from the roof beam and put a ladder up against the beam. I hoisted the box up into the rafters and then holding the rope tight I slowly went up the ladder. When I got to the top, there was the box dangling from the rope and I had to fit it onto the brackets I had already put up. To do this I tied the end of the rope onto the ladder to hold it. I then realised that I had forgotten the screwdriver so I went down the ladder but as I got off it, the ladder went up as the box came crashing down...

Epilogue

And it is still happening…during the proof reading of this book, this happened.

The Swiss Cheese

It was going to be a simple flying trip. I just had to drive to the airfield where they maintain my aircraft to fly it back to my home airfield after its annual service. Freddy would then fly me back to collect my car in his aeroplane and then I would drive home. Freddy would just fly back to our home airfield – simple. But then there is the case of the Swiss cheese. This theory states that if all the holes in the cheese line up, then an accident will happen. If one of the holes does not line up, then an accident would be avoided.

The weather was stiflingly hot and my car's thermometer was showing 32degrees. There were a few puffy cumulus clouds at high level and the visibility was crystal clear. It had been a scorcher of a summer so far with the temperatures averaging 30 degrees with hardly any rain. Everything was hot to the touch.

The maintenance airfield has two runways both east-west. One is hard tarmac and the other is grass. The wind was westerly about 10 knots, so I lined up on the westerly hard runway. Being very hot, I assumed that the engine power would be down. However, as I started to accelerate down the runway, the aircraft left the ground after only a very short run and climbed very quickly. The flight back to my home base was very smooth.

On final approach to the runway I cut the power, but my aircraft did not seem to be descending. I came over the threshold still too high, so I put on 40 degrees of flap. Still she would not come down and she should be dropping like a stone. I eventually made a good landing and taxied back to the apron where I park her. When I studied other landing aircraft, they were all having the same problem. I came to the conclusion that the heat from the ground was causing the air to rise rapidly and was keeping the aircraft up. – **Swiss Cheese Hole Number 1**

Freddy had recently taken a share in a nippy little sports aircraft and had been visiting a great number of small grass airfields and posting them on Facebook. He is a very good pilot and he had taken me to a small airfield in Norfolk a few months previously. His aircraft can get into very small strips and in Norfolk he landed it within a few metres. He had become very confident in the aircraft and as it turned out a bit too complacent. – **Swiss Cheese Hole Number 2**

Although Freddy had told the airfield operator to get his aircraft out of the hanger, it was still inside behind a large aircraft. This annoyed Freddy a bit but it was soon out and prepared to go. He was then told that they had filled up the tanks of his aircraft and unbeknown to me, Freddy thought, *Ah we might be a bit overweight*, as we had two up, full tanks and both had flight bags. Afterwards, we calculated that it was 50Kg overweight. – **Swiss Cheese Hole Number 3**

Freddy said that he had not been to my maintenance airfield before as he never liked the look of the runways. He did not know why but had avoided going there when he had a larger aircraft. He later told me that this was on his mind all the time of the flight. – **Swiss Cheese Hole Number 4**.

When we left our airfield the wind direction was all over the place but only very light. The actual flight would only last for about 15 minutes and halfway there, I told Freddy about the hot air rising and making the aircraft float along the runway. I also explained about landing at the maintenance airfield. I told him that the wind was westerly when I left so we should land on the westerly runway. I also explained about the circuit pattern and how he should fly over a golf course and then turn on final approach. I told him that he should watch out for the high electric pylons and the busy road on the runway threshold. I was convinced that the wind had not changed and that it was still westerly. – **Swiss Cheese Hole Number 5**.

As Freddy turned onto final approach, I mentioned that he was a bit high and not to worry too much about the pylons as they were only 100 foot high. He then told me that he would take the grass runway rather than the nice smooth tarmac one. – **Swiss Cheese Hole Number 6.**

As we flew over the pylons, I told him he was still too high and to reduce height. He cut the engine revs but it was still not coming down very quickly. He lowered the nose, but this just put the speed up too high. – **Swiss Cheese Hole Number 7.**

The owner of the airfield who witnessed the event later told me that the windsock was still, until we were on final approach when it decided to swing round from the east. We were therefore landing with a tailwind. This would increase our already fast approach. – **Swiss Cheese Hole Number 8.**

And then it happened…

Freddy touched down on the grass runway too fast, the aircraft hit a bump and we were flying again, we landed again and hit another bump, we were flying again, then landed and rose again and again, we were running out of runway fast. One more bump and we were at the windsock at the end of the runway so at last Freddy decided to go around, still with full flap. The hedge running next to a road was looming fast in the windscreen and as the aircraft dragged itself into the air it pitched to the left towards a hanger. We were about to stall and spin in. All I could see in the windscreen was the huge hanger. Freddy managed to correct it at the last second and we missed the hanger and lurched over the hedge by just a few feet. We skimmed over the fields beyond, where, luckily the crop had been harvested, and finally climbed away.

We climbed up to circuit height and did an about turn after we realised the wind was in the opposite direction. Freddy made a perfect landing and stopped within a few feet. We taxied near to the windsock and discussed the Swiss cheese holes and how they all lined up into a disaster. That aircraft should have crashed but why didn't it?

Not enough airspeed, full flap, no runway left, a hanger and a hedge in the way, very hot weather, overweight and a tailwind.

Only one hole did not line up…it must have been my lifelong favourite friend…

My Guardian Angel